Home Hustle Harmony: Unlocking Your Work-From-Home Wealth

Aura Marx

INTRODUCTION

Welcome to a comprehensive exploration designed for the modern entrepreneur who seeks to navigate the complexities and embrace the opportunities of working from home. In an era where remote work has transcended trend to become a mainstay, "Home Hustle Harmony: Unlocking Your Work-From-Home Wealth" offers a step-by-step guide to setting up, scaling, and flourishing in a home-based business. This book is more than just a manual; it's a companion for the journey, crafted with the understanding that the path of entrepreneurship is as rewarding as it is challenging.

Within these pages, we delve into the essential facets of home-based entrepreneurship, from laying the foundational stones of business planning and financial management to navigating the intricacies of digital marketing and community building. Each chapter is designed to equip you with the tools, knowledge, and insights necessary to thrive in a competitive landscape, ensuring your venture is not just sustainable but also capable of growth and innovation.

"Home Hustle Harmony" is more than a guide; it's a testament to the resilience, creativity, and indomitable spirit of entrepreneurs like you, who dare to dream and work towards making those dreams a reality from the comfort of their homes. Let's embark on this journey together, turning challenges into stepping stones and aspirations into achievements.

Table of Contents

Chapter 1: The New Era of Work

Introduction to the evolving work landscape

In the opening of our journey into "Home Hustle Harmony: Unlocking Your Work-From-Home Wealth," we embark on an exploration of the transformative shifts in the global work landscape. The very fabric of what we consider 'work' has undergone a radical metamorphosis, particularly in the last decade, a change accelerated by technological advancements and, more recently, the global pandemic.
Gone are the days when work was synonymous with a physical office space, a 9-to-5 schedule, and the daily commute. We've witnessed a seismic shift towards a more flexible, digital-first approach, where the lines between home and office blur. This evolution isn't just about where we work, but also how we work, who we work with, and what work means to us.

The Digital Revolution: At the heart of this change is the digital revolution. The internet, smartphones, cloud computing, and a plethora of productivity tools have made it possible to work from virtually anywhere. This democratization of work access has opened up new opportunities, especially for Millennials and Gen Z, who are digital natives, valuing flexibility, autonomy, and purpose in their careers.

The Rise of the Gig Economy: Parallel to technological advancements, the gig economy has flourished, characterized by freelance work, flexible hours, and project-based tasks. This shift towards a more project-centric work model has empowered individuals to take control of their careers, pick projects that resonate with their skills and interests, and design a work-life blend that suits their lifestyle.

The Pandemic's Impact: The COVID-19 pandemic served as a catalyst, forcing businesses and individuals worldwide to adopt remote work almost overnight. This unplanned global experiment not only demonstrated the viability of remote work but also reshaped perceptions of productivity, collaboration, and the essence of work-life balance. It highlighted the potential for remote work to be not just a necessity but a preferred mode of operation for many.

A New Understanding of Productivity: The evolving work landscape has ushered in a new understanding of productivity. It's no longer just about the hours spent at a desk but about the output and the impact of the work done. This has led to a greater emphasis on results, empowering individuals to craft their schedules around when and how they work best, fostering a culture of trust and accountability.

The Importance of Community and Connection: Despite the physical distance, there's a growing emphasis on building virtual communities and connections. Digital tools have enabled networking, collaboration, and social interaction, ensuring that the human aspect of work remains vibrant and fulfilling.

As we delve deeper into "Home Hustle Harmony," we'll explore how these changes form the backdrop of a thriving home-based business environment. We'll uncover strategies to leverage this evolving work landscape to build a profitable, balanced, and fulfilling work-from-home life. This journey is about embracing change, harnessing technology, and redefining what success looks like in the modern world of work.

The Rise of Remote Work and Its Potential

The ascent of remote work is more than just a trend; it's a fundamental shift in the paradigm of employment and entrepreneurship. This movement away from traditional office environments towards a more distributed workforce has been building momentum over the years, propelled by technological advancements and a growing emphasis on work-life balance. The potential of remote work to reshape industries, empower individuals, and redefine productivity is immense.

Technological Enablers: At the forefront of this shift are the technological enablers that have made remote work not just feasible but efficient. High-speed internet, cloud computing, and collaborative tools like video conferencing, project management apps, and instant messaging have bridged the gap between physical presence and virtual collaboration. These tools have not only facilitated communication but also ensured that teamwork and project management remain seamless, regardless of geographical boundaries.

Flexibility and Autonomy: One of the most appealing aspects of remote work is the flexibility it offers. Individuals gain control over their schedules, allowing them to work during their most productive hours, balance personal commitments, and reduce the time and stress associated with commuting. This autonomy supports a more personalized work experience, where employees can tailor their environment, schedule, and work style to suit their preferences and needs.

Access to a Global Talent Pool: For businesses, remote work opens up a global talent pool, unbounded by geographic limitations. This access to a diverse range of skills and perspectives can drive innovation, cultural richness, and competitive advantage. Companies can find the best fit for their needs, regardless of where the individual resides, making it a win-win for both employers and employees.

Sustainability and Cost Savings: Remote work also offers significant sustainability benefits and cost savings. Reduced commuting and office space needs lower the carbon footprint and operational expenses. For individuals, this translates to savings on travel costs, work attire, and other expenses associated with a traditional office job. For companies, the reduction in overhead can lead to more investment in growth, employee benefits, and innovation.

Empowerment through Entrepreneurship: The rise of remote work is closely linked to the surge in home-based businesses and entrepreneurship. The barriers to entry for starting a business have significantly lowered, allowing more people to pursue their entrepreneurial dreams. From e-commerce stores to digital services, the potential to build and grow a business from the comfort of one's home has never been more accessible.

Challenges and Opportunities: While remote work offers numerous benefits, it also presents challenges such as isolation, overwork, and the need for discipline and self-motivation. Addressing these challenges is essential for individuals and organizations to fully harness the potential of remote work. Creating virtual communities, establishing clear boundaries, and developing robust support systems are crucial for maintaining well-being and productivity.

As we navigate through this chapter, we will delve deeper into how individuals and businesses can leverage the opportunities presented by remote work. We will explore strategies for maximizing productivity, fostering community, and ensuring a healthy balance between professional and personal life. The potential of remote work is not just in its ability to transform where we work, but in its power to enrich how we work, live, and interact in this increasingly digital world.

Understanding Millennials and Gen Z

In the evolving tapestry of the modern workforce, Millennials and Generation Z stand out for their unique characteristics, values, and expectations from work and life. These generations are not just shaping the future of work; they are redefining it. To truly harness the potential of remote work and entrepreneurship, it's crucial to delve deep into understanding these dynamic groups.

Millennials: The Pioneers of Change

Born between the early 1980s and the mid-1990s, Millennials have been the torchbearers of the digital revolution. Having come of age during the internet boom, this generation has been at the forefront of blending technology with daily life. They witnessed the transition from dial-up internet to high-speed broadband, from desktop computers to smartphones, making them adaptable, tech-savvy, and open to new ways of working.

Millennials value flexibility, purpose, and work-life integration. They are not just looking for a job; they are seeking careers that offer meaningful work, opportunities for growth, and alignment with their personal values. This generation has spearheaded the gig economy, favoring freelance opportunities, and remote roles that offer autonomy and the chance to balance multiple interests and responsibilities.

However, they also face unique challenges. Many entered the job market during the economic downturns of the early 2000s and 2010s, which has shaped their approach to financial stability, job security, and entrepreneurship. They are highly educated yet burdened with student debt, making the prospect of traditional 9-to-5 jobs less appealing and pushing many towards innovative career paths, including starting their own businesses.

Generation Z: Digital Natives Redefining Norms

Following the Millennials, Generation Z, born from the mid-1990s to the early 2010s, is the first generation to grow up entirely in the digital age. For them, technology is not just a tool; it's an integral part of their existence. This has made Gen Z exceptionally comfortable with digital platforms, online communication, and virtual collaboration.

Gen Z values authenticity, diversity, and inclusivity. They are more pragmatic and financially minded than their predecessors, having grown up during the global financial crisis and the pandemic. They seek stability but not at the cost of their well-being or personal values. This generation is more entrepreneurial, with a strong desire to impact the world positively, making them more inclined to pursue ventures that align with their ethical and environmental values.

For Gen Z, the concept of a traditional career path is even less appealing than it was for Millennials. They are drawn to flexible, project-based work that allows them to express their creativity, learn new skills, and collaborate with diverse teams. They are also more concerned with mental health and seek a work environment that supports their well-being.

Adapting to the Needs of Millennials and Gen Z

To engage these generations in the realm of remote work and entrepreneurship, it's essential to understand their need for flexibility, purpose, and inclusivity. Work opportunities that offer a blend of autonomy, personal growth, and community engagement are particularly appealing. Providing clear paths for advancement, continuous learning opportunities, and platforms for collaboration can help in attracting and retaining talent from these groups.

Moreover, Millennials and Gen Z are looking for transparency, ethical practices, and social responsibility in their work environments. Businesses that prioritize sustainability, community involvement, and equitable practices will find a more receptive audience among these younger generations.

In terms of entrepreneurship, Millennials and Gen Z are not just looking to start any business; they want to build ventures that reflect their values, address societal issues, and contribute to the greater good. They are more likely to support and engage with brands that have a clear mission and purpose beyond profit.

Embracing a New Work Ethic

The work ethic of Millennials and Gen Z is characterized by a desire for balance, meaning, and connection. They are redefining success, not by the traditional metrics of title and wealth, but by the impact they make and the quality of their lives. Remote work and entrepreneurship offer the canvas for these generations to paint their vision of a fulfilling career, blending their professional aspirations with their personal values and lifestyles.
As we delve deeper into understanding Millennials and Gen Z, it becomes clear that the future of work is not just about where we work, but how we work. It's about creating environments that foster innovation, inclusivity, and well-being. It's about building businesses that are not only profitable but also purpose-driven and sustainable. By tapping into the aspirations, values, and skills of these generations, we can unlock a new era of work that is more adaptable, equitable, and fulfilling for everyone.

Chapter 2: Laying the Foundations

Mindset for success in work-from-home ventures

Transitioning to or starting a work-from-home venture requires more than just a physical shift from an office to a home environment; it necessitates a profound transformation in mindset. The success of remote work hinges not only on external factors like technology and workspace but, more critically, on the internal landscape of one's attitudes, beliefs, and mental resilience. Cultivating the right mindset is the bedrock upon which the edifice of home-based success is built.

Embracing Autonomy and Responsibility
At the heart of the work-from-home paradigm lies the principle of autonomy. This freedom is both liberating and demanding, as it comes with the responsibility of self-management. Success in a remote setting requires the cultivation of self-discipline and the ability to self-motivate. The absence of traditional office structures and immediate oversight means that individuals must internalize their work ethic, setting and adhering to their schedules, deadlines, and quality standards.

Cultivating a Growth Mindset
A growth mindset, as popularized by psychologist Carol Dweck, is pivotal for remote workers and entrepreneurs. This perspective thrives on challenges, views failures as learning opportunities, and embraces continuous improvement. In the dynamic landscape of remote work, where roles, technologies, and market demands are constantly evolving, a growth mindset empowers individuals to adapt, learn new skills, and remain resilient in the face of setbacks.

Building Resilience and Adaptability
The nature of working from home, coupled with the entrepreneurial journey, is replete with uncertainties and fluctuations. Building resilience—the capacity to recover from

difficulties—and adaptability—the ability to adjust to new conditions—is crucial. This means maintaining a positive outlook, managing stress effectively, and being prepared to pivot strategies when circumstances change. Resilience and adaptability are not innate traits but skills that can be developed through mindfulness practices, stress management techniques, and a supportive network.

Fostering a Strong Work Ethic
A robust work ethic is characterized by dedication, integrity, and professionalism. It involves showing up for your work with the same seriousness and commitment you would bring to an external office. This includes maintaining regular work hours, delivering high-quality work consistently, and communicating effectively with clients or team members. It's about honoring commitments and exceeding expectations, even when no one is watching.

Prioritizing Work-Life Balance
One of the paradoxes of remote work is that while it offers the flexibility to blend work and life seamlessly, it can also lead to the blurring of boundaries between the two, often tilting towards overwork. Successful remote workers and entrepreneurs recognize the importance of work-life balance for long-term sustainability. This involves setting clear boundaries between work and personal time, creating routines that delineate the workday's start and end, and ensuring time is allocated for rest, recreation, and relationships.

Developing Effective Communication Skills
Remote work relies heavily on written and virtual communication, making it imperative to develop clear and effective communication skills. This encompasses not only the ability to convey ideas and instructions succinctly but also the skill to listen actively and empathize with team members or clients from diverse backgrounds. Emotional intelligence plays a significant role here,

enabling individuals to navigate the nuances of remote interactions, where the absence of physical cues can lead to misunderstandings.

Nurturing a Network and Community
The isolation that can sometimes accompany remote work underscores the importance of building a network and a sense of community. This involves engaging with professional networks, participating in virtual meetups, and possibly joining or forming support groups with other remote workers or entrepreneurs. Such communities can provide not only camaraderie and moral support but also opportunities for collaboration, learning, and growth.

Embracing Continuous Learning
The landscape of remote work and entrepreneurship is continually evolving, driven by technological advancements and changing market dynamics. A mindset geared towards continuous learning is essential to stay relevant and competitive. This means staying abreast of industry trends, upskilling, and being open to feedback and new ideas.

Cultivating a mindset for success in work-from-home ventures is a multifaceted endeavor. It involves a blend of self-discipline, resilience, continuous improvement, and effective communication, all underpinned by a clear sense of purpose and well-being. By nurturing these internal attributes, individuals can not only thrive in their remote work and entrepreneurial endeavors but also contribute to a more flexible, inclusive, and dynamic future of work.

Essential tools and technology for a home office

In the realm of remote work and home-based entrepreneurship, the significance of equipping oneself with the right tools and technology cannot be overstated. These digital and physical assets form the backbone of productivity, efficiency, and connectivity, transforming any space into a potent hub of professional activity. Here, we delve into the essential tools and technologies that are pivotal for setting up a functional and effective home office.

Reliable High-Speed Internet Connection
The cornerstone of any remote work setup is a robust and reliable high-speed internet connection. Given the critical nature of online communication, cloud-based services, and data transfer in remote work, a fast and stable internet connection ensures that work processes are smooth and uninterrupted. It's advisable to invest in a plan that offers adequate speed and bandwidth to support video conferencing, large file uploads/downloads, and simultaneous use of multiple online tools.

Ergonomic Workspace Design
Creating an ergonomic workspace is crucial for long-term comfort and health. This includes a quality office chair that supports proper posture, an adjustable desk (consider a standing desk option for flexibility), adequate lighting to reduce eye strain, and a monitor at eye level to prevent neck pain. An ergonomically designed keyboard and mouse can also help prevent repetitive strain injuries. The physical setup of a home office should promote productivity while safeguarding health.

High-Performance Computer or Laptop
The choice of computing hardware, whether a desktop or a laptop, should be dictated by the nature of the work, required software, and personal preference for mobility. A high-performance computer with a fast processor, sufficient RAM, and ample storage is essential for handling multitasking, running complex programs, and ensuring smooth operation. Regular updates and maintenance are also vital to keep the system running efficiently.

Productivity and Collaboration Software
A suite of productivity and collaboration software is indispensable for remote work. This includes word processing, spreadsheets, and presentation tools, as well as project management and collaboration platforms like Asana, Trello, or Slack. These tools facilitate task management, team communication, and project tracking, keeping everyone aligned and productive.

Communication Tools
Effective communication tools are the lifeline of remote work, bridging the gap between distributed teams and clients. Video conferencing tools like Zoom, Microsoft Teams, or Google Meet are essential for virtual meetings, providing a more personal connection than emails or phone calls. Email remains a staple for formal communications, while instant messaging apps offer quick, informal interaction.

Data Storage and Backup Solutions
Data security and management are paramount in a home office setup. Cloud storage services like Google Drive, Dropbox, or OneDrive offer secure and accessible storage options, facilitating file sharing and collaboration. Additionally, having a reliable backup system, including external hard drives and regular cloud backups, ensures that data is safe and recoverable in case of hardware failure or other issues.

Cybersecurity Measures
With the increasing threat of cyber-attacks, protecting sensitive information and maintaining privacy is crucial. A robust antivirus software, a reliable VPN (Virtual Private Network), and strong, regularly updated passwords are foundational cybersecurity measures. Awareness of phishing scams and regular software updates further bolster security.

Auxiliary Devices and Accessories

Depending on the nature of the work, additional devices and accessories may enhance productivity and ease of tasks. This could include a high-quality webcam and microphone for clearer video calls, a noise-canceling headset for focus, a second monitor for extended screen real estate, and a reliable printer/scanner if dealing with physical documents.

Personalization for Maximum Efficiency

Beyond these essentials, personalizing the home office with items that enhance productivity and well-being—like a whiteboard for brainstorming, plants for a touch of nature, or even a comfortable area for breaks—can significantly impact daily work life. The goal is to create an environment that not only meets professional needs but also inspires and motivates.

Equipping a home office with the right tools and technology is a dynamic process, evolving with the changing needs of the remote worker or entrepreneur. By investing in a solid foundation of essential tools and staying adaptable to incorporate new innovations, individuals can create a home office that is not just a space to work but a catalyst for success, creativity, and growth in the digital age.

Setting clear goals and expectations

In the journey of establishing a successful work-from-home venture, the act of setting clear goals and expectations emerges as a pivotal compass. This practice not only delineates the path to be traversed but also serves as a beacon, guiding through the ebbs and flows of remote work dynamics. The articulation of precise objectives and the establishment of transparent expectations are instrumental in fostering a sense of direction, motivation, and accountability, both for individuals and teams navigating the remote work landscape.

Defining Vision and Objectives
The genesis of goal setting begins with a clear vision—a vivid picture of what one aspires to achieve through their work-from-home endeavor. This vision should encapsulate both the broader aspirations and the specific objectives that constitute the steps toward realizing this dream. Whether it's achieving financial independence, creating a flexible lifestyle, or making a tangible impact within a chosen field, the vision sets the stage for more detailed goal-setting.

SMART Goal Framework

The SMART framework offers a robust structure for goal formulation, ensuring that objectives are Specific, Measurable, Achievable, Relevant, and Time-bound. Applying this framework compels a deep dive into the specifics of each goal, encouraging a breakdown into quantifiable targets, realistic timelines, and actionable steps. For instance, rather than a vague aim to "increase business revenue," a SMART goal would specify "to increase revenue by 20% within the next quarter through expanding the service offerings and optimizing marketing strategies."

Aligning Goals with Personal and Professional Values
In the realm of remote work, where the lines between personal and professional life often blur, it's crucial that goals resonate with one's values and life vision. This alignment ensures that the pursuit of professional objectives does not come at the expense of personal well-being or values but rather complements and enriches the overall quality of life. Goals that align with personal values foster intrinsic motivation, making the journey toward them more fulfilling and sustainable.

Setting Milestones and Benchmarks
Breaking down overarching goals into smaller, manageable milestones and benchmarks facilitates progress tracking and maintains momentum. These waypoints serve as indicators of progress, offering opportunities for reflection, adjustment, and celebration of achievements along the way. Milestones also help in identifying potential roadblocks early, allowing for timely interventions and course corrections.

Establishing Clear Expectations
Beyond personal goal setting, clear expectations are paramount in the context of remote teamwork and client relationships. This involves defining roles, responsibilities, communication protocols, and deliverables upfront, minimizing ambiguities and potential misunderstandings. In a remote setting, where face-to-face interactions are limited, the clarity of expectations becomes the glue that holds collaborative efforts together.

Feedback Loops and Continuous Evaluation
The dynamic nature of remote work and the fast-paced environments many home-based businesses operate in demand regular evaluation of goals and performance. Establishing feedback loops with team members, mentors, and clients provides valuable insights and perspectives that can inform goal reassessment and refinement. This iterative process ensures that goals remain relevant and aligned with changing circumstances and growth trajectories.

Balancing Ambition with Well-being
In the pursuit of professional goals, it's imperative to maintain a balance that safeguards physical and mental well-being. Setting realistic goals that challenge yet do not overwhelm is key. Incorporating goals related to self-care, mental health, and leisure ensures that the zeal for achievement is balanced with the need for rejuvenation and personal fulfillment.

Visualization and Affirmation
The power of visualization and positive affirmations in goal achievement cannot be understated. Envisioning the successful attainment of goals and regularly affirming one's ability to achieve them can bolster confidence and motivation. This mental practice complements the tangible steps taken toward goals, reinforcing the belief in one's potential and the possibility of desired outcomes.

In sum, setting clear goals and expectations in a work-from-home context is a multifaceted endeavor that extends beyond mere task completion. It's about crafting a vision that integrates professional aspirations with personal values, breaking down this vision into actionable objectives, and navigating the path with clarity, purpose, and adaptability. This structured approach not only propels one toward their desired outcomes but also enriches the journey, making it a rewarding experience of growth, learning, and self-discovery.

Chapter 3: Designing Your Home Hustle

Identifying profitable niches suited to work-from-home

In the landscape of work-from-home ventures, the identification of a profitable niche is akin to discovering a vein of gold in the vast mine of opportunities. It's the sweet spot where personal passion, market demand, and the potential for profitability converge. Navigating this terrain requires a blend of introspection, market research, and strategic thinking. By delving into the depths of various industries and market trends, one can unearth niches that not only promise financial rewards but also resonate on a personal level, offering a fulfilling path to entrepreneurial success.

Self-Assessment and Skill Inventory

The quest for the right niche begins with a mirror into one's skills, interests, and experiences. This introspective journey involves cataloging one's abilities, passions, and areas of expertise to identify potential areas where these elements align. Whether it's a knack for digital marketing, a flair for design, or a deep understanding of health and wellness, each individual possesses a unique set of skills and interests that can serve as a compass in the niche selection process.

Market Demand and Trends Analysis

With a clear understanding of personal strengths and interests, the next step involves scanning the market landscape to identify trends and demands that align with one's skill set. This involves keeping a pulse on emerging industries, consumer behavior changes, and technological advancements. Tools like Google Trends, industry reports, and social media platforms can offer insights into what products or services are gaining traction, where there are gaps in the market, and what consumers are currently interested in.

Competition and Saturation Evaluation
While a high demand for a particular niche is promising, it's also crucial to assess the level of competition and market saturation. A highly competitive niche may require significant efforts and resources to stand out, whereas a less saturated niche might offer easier entry points but potentially lower demand. The key is to find a balance, looking for niches where there is enough demand to ensure profitability but not so much competition that it becomes prohibitive to make a mark.

Profitability and Monetization Potential
Not all interests or passions can be easily monetized. It's essential to evaluate the profitability of a niche by considering factors like pricing potential, recurring revenue opportunities, and the cost of delivering the product or service. Some niches might offer higher average transaction values, while others could provide steady income through subscription models or repeat purchases. This financial lens helps to focus on niches that not only align with personal and market interests but also have a clear path to financial sustainability.

Adaptability and Future Growth
In the dynamic digital landscape, the longevity of a niche is as important as its current profitability. It's wise to choose niches that show potential for adaptation and growth. This could mean selecting areas that are likely to evolve with technological advancements, have the potential to expand into new markets, or can adapt to changing consumer preferences. A niche that is too narrow or tied to fleeting trends might offer short-term gains but could falter as the market evolves.

Validation through Testing and Feedback
Before fully committing to a niche, it's prudent to validate its viability through testing and obtaining feedback. This could involve creating a minimal viable product (MVP), offering a pilot service, or conducting market surveys. Feedback from potential customers

can provide invaluable insights into the demand, pricing sensitivity, and potential improvements, reducing the risk of venturing into a non-viable niche.

Building on Niches with Personal Meaning
While profitability is a critical factor in niche selection, incorporating personal meaning and passion into the equation can lead to greater fulfillment and resilience. A niche that aligns with one's values and interests is more likely to inspire persistence, creativity, and dedication, especially when faced with the inevitable challenges of entrepreneurship.

Identifying a profitable niche suited to work-from-home ventures is a multifaceted process that intertwines personal introspection with market intelligence. It's about finding a harmony between what one loves to do, what one is good at, and what the market needs. This delicate balance, when struck, paves the way for not only financial success but also personal satisfaction and growth, laying a solid foundation for a thriving home-based business.

Basics of business planning and model design

Embarking on a work-from-home venture without a roadmap is akin to navigating uncharted waters without a compass. Business planning and model design serve as the navigational tools that guide entrepreneurs through the complexities of establishing and growing a home-based business. These foundational elements are crucial in translating an idea into a viable enterprise, ensuring that the vision, goals, and operational strategies are clearly defined, aligned, and actionable.
Crafting a Comprehensive Business Plan

The cornerstone of any successful business endeavor is a well-constructed business plan. This document is more than just a requirement for seeking financing; it's a strategic blueprint that outlines the journey from concept to market reality. A comprehensive business plan covers several key components:

Executive Summary: This section provides a snapshot of the business, encapsulating the mission statement, business model, primary products or services, target market, and financial highlights. It's the elevator pitch of the business plan, designed to captivate and inform.

Market Analysis: An in-depth market analysis delves into understanding the industry landscape, target customer segments, market needs, and competitive environment. This analysis informs the business strategy, highlighting opportunities for differentiation and competitive advantage.

Organization and Management: Detailing the business structure, management team, and operational logistics, this section outlines how the business will be run, who will be involved, and what roles they will play. For home-based businesses, it may also address how to effectively manage remote work dynamics.

Products or Services: This part of the plan describes the offerings in detail, explaining the benefits, features, and unique selling propositions. It should also address the product lifecycle, development roadmap, and any intellectual property considerations.

Marketing and Sales Strategy: A robust marketing and sales strategy is vital for attracting and retaining customers. This section outlines the channels, tactics, and tools that will be used to reach the target market, along with pricing, sales processes, and customer service approaches.

Financial Projections: Financial planning is critical for assessing the viability and sustainability of the business. This includes detailed projections for revenue, expenses, cash flow, and profitability, alongside scenarios for best and worst-case financial outcomes.

Funding Request (if applicable): For businesses seeking external funding, this section specifies the amount of funding needed, its intended use, and the proposed terms for repayment or equity exchange.

Designing an Agile Business Model

The business model is the mechanism through which the business creates, delivers, and captures value. In the context of work-from-home ventures, where agility and adaptability are paramount, designing a flexible and scalable business model is crucial.

Value Proposition: The heart of the business model is the value proposition, which articulates the unique benefits that the business offers to its customers. This should clearly address the customer's pain points and how the business's offerings provide a solution.

Customer Segments: Identifying and understanding the target customer segments is essential for tailoring the value proposition, marketing efforts, and product development to meet their specific needs and preferences.

Channels: This aspect of the business model outlines how the business will reach its customers and deliver its value proposition. For home-based businesses, digital channels such as e-commerce platforms, social media, and email marketing often play a significant role.

The most popular channels include:

Social Media Platforms: Sites like Facebook, Instagram, Twitter, LinkedIn, and Pinterest are powerful for engaging with customers, building brand awareness, and driving traffic to websites or online stores. They offer targeted advertising options based on user demographics, interests, and behaviors.

Search Engine Optimization (SEO): Optimizing website content to rank higher in search engine results pages (SERPs) for relevant keywords helps attract organic traffic. This involves both on-page optimization (like keyword integration, meta tags, and content quality) and off-page optimization (such as backlinking and social signals).

Content Marketing: Creating valuable content (blogs, videos, infographics, podcasts) that resonates with the target audience can attract and retain customers. Content marketing is effective for establishing authority, improving SEO, and engaging users at various stages of the customer journey.

Email Marketing: Despite being one of the oldest online marketing channels, email marketing remains highly effective for personalized communication, customer retention, and direct sales promotions. Building a subscriber list and sending regular newsletters, offers, and updates can drive significant engagement and conversions.

Pay-Per-Click (PPC) Advertising: Platforms like Google AdWords and Bing Ads allow businesses to display ads in search engine results and on partner websites. Advertisers pay only when their ads are clicked, making PPC a direct and controllable way to drive traffic.

Affiliate Marketing: Partnering with individuals or other businesses to promote products or services in exchange for a commission on sales or leads generated. Affiliate marketing extends the reach of online businesses through the networks of their affiliates.

Influencer Marketing: Collaborating with influencers who have a significant following on social media or other platforms can boost brand visibility and credibility. Influencers can create sponsored content that introduces products or services to their audience.

Marketplaces and E-commerce Platforms: Selling products on established online marketplaces like Amazon, eBay, Etsy, or using e-commerce platforms like Shopify or WooCommerce, can provide access to large audiences and streamlined selling processes.

Online Webinars and Workshops: Hosting informative webinars, workshops, or live sessions can attract potential customers interested in a particular topic, product, or service. These can be used for lead generation and establishing expertise in a field.

Display Advertising: Using banner ads, video ads, or interactive media on relevant websites or ad networks can increase brand exposure and attract traffic. Display advertising can be targeted based on user behavior, website content, and more.

Mobile Marketing: Reaching customers through mobile-specific channels like SMS marketing, mobile apps, or mobile-optimized websites caters to the growing number of users who primarily use smartphones for internet access.

Video Marketing: Platforms like YouTube offer a vast audience for video content, which can be used for tutorials, product reviews, brand storytelling, and more. Video content tends to have high engagement rates and can improve SEO as well.

Each of these channels can be utilized based on the specific business model, target audience, and marketing objectives. Often, a combination of several channels, aligned in a coherent digital marketing strategy, yields the best results for online businesses.

Revenue Streams: A sustainable business model requires clear revenue streams. This could include product sales, service fees, subscription models, affiliate marketing, or a combination of multiple streams.

Cost Structure: Understanding the cost structure is vital for financial planning and management. This includes both fixed costs (e.g., software subscriptions, website hosting) and variable costs (e.g., product manufacturing, shipping) associated with running the business.

Key Partnerships: Strategic partnerships can enhance the business's value proposition, expand its reach, or streamline operations. Identifying potential partners, such as suppliers, distributors, or complementary service providers, is an integral part of the business model design.

In crafting the business plan and designing the business model, the emphasis should be on clarity, realism, and strategic thinking. These documents are not static; they should evolve as the business grows and adapts to changing market conditions. For entrepreneurs embarking on work-from-home ventures, the business plan and model are not just formalities but vital tools for strategic decision-making, risk management, and long-term success.

Legalities and logistics

Navigating the legalities and logistics of setting up a home-based business is a critical step that lays the foundation for a sustainable and compliant operation. This process involves a series of considerations, from choosing the right legal structure to understanding zoning laws, that ensure the business operates within legal boundaries and is set up for long-term success.

Choosing the Right Business Structure

The selection of a business entity has significant implications for taxation, liability, and the ability to raise capital. Common structures for home-based businesses include sole proprietorships, partnerships, limited liability companies (LLCs), and corporations. Each has its advantages and drawbacks, and the choice depends on factors such as the level of personal liability protection desired, tax considerations, and the complexity of the business operations.

Sole Proprietorship: The simplest form, where the business and the owner are legally the same entity. It requires minimal setup but offers no personal liability protection.

Partnership: Similar to a sole proprietorship but involves two or more people. Partners share profits, losses, and responsibilities, and personal liability varies based on the partnership type.

Limited Liability Company (LLC): Combines the flexibility of a partnership with the liability protection of a corporation. It's popular among small businesses for its simplicity and tax advantages.

Corporation: A more complex structure that provides significant liability protection and options for raising capital through stock. However, it involves more regulatory requirements and can be more expensive to establish and maintain.

Business Registration and Licensing

Registering the business with the appropriate local, state, and federal authorities is essential for legality and tax purposes. This process may include obtaining a general business license, specific permits related to the nature of the business (like health permits for food-related businesses), and a sales tax license if selling taxable goods or services.

Zoning Laws and Home-Based Business Regulations

Understanding and complying with local zoning laws is crucial for home-based businesses. These laws dictate what types of business activities can occur in residential areas and may impose restrictions on signage, customer traffic, noise levels, and the percentage of the home used for business purposes. It's important to check with local zoning boards or municipal offices to ensure the home-based business complies with all local ordinances.

Tax Implications and Record-Keeping

Navigating the tax obligations of a home-based business involves understanding which taxes apply (income tax, self-employment tax, sales tax, etc.) and taking advantage of eligible deductions (like the home office deduction). Maintaining meticulous records of income, expenses, and business-related purchases is critical for tax reporting and can aid in maximizing deductions. Consulting with a tax professional can provide tailored advice and ensure compliance with tax laws.

Insurance Considerations

Home-based businesses may need specific insurance policies to cover liabilities not included in standard homeowner's insurance policies. This might include professional liability insurance, product liability insurance, or a business owner's policy that combines several coverages. Assessing the potential risks and consulting with insurance professionals can help determine the appropriate coverage.

Data Protection and Privacy Laws

In today's digital age, protecting customer data is not only ethical but often legally required. Home-based businesses that collect, store, or process personal information must comply with relevant data protection laws, such as the General Data Protection Regulation (GDPR) for businesses dealing with EU citizens or the California Consumer Privacy Act (CCPA) for California residents.

Implementing robust data security practices and understanding the legal obligations regarding data privacy are imperative.

<u>Contractual Agreements and Intellectual Property</u>
For businesses that work with clients, suppliers, or contractors, having well-drafted contracts is essential to define the scope of work, deliverables, payment terms, and dispute resolution mechanisms. Additionally, protecting intellectual property (trademarks, patents, copyrights) can safeguard unique products, services, or branding elements from infringement.

Setting up a home-based business with due diligence to legalities and logistics lays a solid groundwork for operational integrity and risk management. It involves a blend of legal compliance, strategic planning, and administrative organization. By carefully navigating these aspects, entrepreneurs can establish a home-based business that is not only legally sound but poised for growth and success in the competitive market landscape.

Chapter 4: Productivity in Pajamas

Time management and productivity hacks

Mastering time management and productivity is crucial for remote workers who often navigate the challenges of self-discipline, distractions, and the blurring lines between personal and professional life. Adopting effective strategies and hacks can transform the work-from-home experience, enhancing efficiency, reducing stress, and ensuring a healthy work-life balance.

Establishing a Consistent Routine

A consistent daily routine sets the tone for a productive day. Starting with a morning ritual that might include exercise, meditation, or reading can energize and mentally prepare remote workers for the tasks ahead. Structuring the day with set work hours mimics the discipline of a traditional office setting, providing a framework that fosters focus and productivity.

Designating a Dedicated Workspace

Creating a dedicated, distraction-free workspace is vital. This space should be reserved solely for work, equipped with all necessary tools and ergonomic furniture. A well-organized and clutter-free desk can minimize distractions and help in mentally associating this space with professional activities, enhancing focus.

Prioritizing Tasks with the Eisenhower Box

The Eisenhower Box, or Matrix, is a powerful tool for task prioritization, dividing tasks into four categories: urgent and important, important but not urgent, urgent but not important, and neither urgent nor important. This method helps remote workers focus on tasks that contribute significantly to their goals while managing or eliminating less critical tasks.

Implementing the Pomodoro Technique

The Pomodoro Technique involves breaking work into intervals, traditionally 25 minutes in length, separated by short breaks. This method encourages sustained concentration and allows for regular mental refreshment, making it easier to maintain productivity over longer periods.

Leveraging Technology for Efficiency

A plethora of digital tools and apps can streamline workflows and enhance productivity. Task management apps like Asana or Trello provide an overview of tasks and deadlines, while time tracking tools like Toggl or RescueTime offer insights into how work hours are spent, highlighting areas for improvement.

Setting Realistic Goals and Deadlines

Establishing clear, achievable goals and setting realistic deadlines for each task can create a sense of urgency and progress. This practice helps in maintaining momentum and provides a roadmap for the day, ensuring that important tasks are tackled with priority.

Batching Similar Tasks

Grouping similar tasks together can reduce the mental load of switching between different types of activities, conserving energy and increasing efficiency. For instance, dedicating specific blocks of time to emails, calls, creative work, or administrative tasks can streamline the work process and enhance focus.

Managing Distractions Proactively

Proactively managing potential distractions is key for remote workers. This might involve setting boundaries with housemates or family during work hours, using apps to block distracting websites, or setting the phone to "Do Not Disturb" mode during deep work sessions.

Incorporating Regular Breaks
Regular breaks are essential for maintaining mental and physical well-being. Short breaks throughout the day can prevent burnout, boost creativity, and improve concentration. Techniques like the 20-20-20 rule, where every 20 minutes, you look at something 20 feet away for 20 seconds, can help reduce eye strain from screen time.

Practicing Effective Communication
Clear and concise communication with team members and managers is crucial in a remote setting. Regular check-ins, updates, and the use of collaborative tools ensure that everyone is aligned and that expectations are clearly understood, reducing the need for time-consuming corrections and misunderstandings.

Continuous Self-Reflection and Adjustment
Finally, continuous self-reflection on what works and what doesn't allows for ongoing adjustments to work habits and strategies. Personal productivity is not one-size-fits-all; what works for one person may not work for another. Regularly assessing and tweaking time management and productivity approaches can lead to a customized strategy that perfectly suits an individual's work style and preferences.

By integrating these time management and productivity hacks into their daily routine, remote workers can navigate the challenges of working from home more effectively, turning potential distractions and flexibility into assets for high productivity and job satisfaction.

Scan this QR Code for a little gift

Creating and maintaining a productive home workspace

The transition to working from home brings the unique challenge of creating a space that not only fosters productivity but also supports well-being. A thoughtfully designed home workspace can significantly impact focus, creativity, and efficiency. This chapter explores essential considerations and practical tips for setting up and maintaining an environment conducive to high productivity.

Choosing the Right Location

The first step in creating a productive home workspace is selecting an optimal location. Ideally, this should be a quiet area with minimal foot traffic, away from household distractions. Natural light is a significant asset, as it boosts mood and energy levels. If space allows, a separate room dedicated to work can create a clear boundary between professional and personal life, enhancing work-life balance.

Ergonomic Furniture and Equipment

Investing in ergonomic furniture is crucial for comfort and health. An adjustable chair that supports proper posture and a desk at the correct height are fundamental. If possible, consider a standing desk or an adjustable converter to alternate between sitting and standing, reducing the risks associated with prolonged sitting.

An ergonomic keyboard and mouse, positioned to allow for a natural hand posture, can help prevent strain injuries. Additionally, ensuring the computer monitor is at eye level and at an appropriate distance can reduce eye strain and neck discomfort.

Organized and Clutter-Free Environment

A clutter-free workspace promotes clarity and focus. Organizational tools like shelving units, desk organizers, and cable management solutions can keep the workspace tidy and functional. Regularly decluttering the desk and digital desktop can help maintain a conducive work environment, minimizing distractions and making it easier to find necessary tools and documents.

Personalizing the Space
While functionality is paramount, personalizing the workspace with elements that inspire and motivate can enhance productivity and job satisfaction. This might include plants, which can improve air quality and mood, artwork or motivational quotes, and personal mementos that bring joy and inspiration.

Optimal Lighting and Ventilation
Good lighting is essential to prevent eye strain and maintain energy levels. If possible, set up the workspace to take advantage of natural light, complemented by task lighting, such as a desk lamp, to ensure the work area is well-lit regardless of the time of day.

Adequate ventilation and comfortable temperature control are also important for maintaining focus and comfort. An air purifier can improve air quality, especially in areas with limited ventilation.

Technology and Connectivity
Ensuring reliable technology and connectivity is a cornerstone of a productive home workspace. This includes a high-speed internet connection, sufficient data storage solutions, and access to necessary software and applications. Backup solutions, such as an external hard drive or cloud storage, are essential for data security.

Noise Management
Controlling noise levels is crucial, especially in busy households or noisy neighborhoods. Noise-cancelling headphones can be invaluable for maintaining concentration. Alternatively, white noise

machines or apps can mask distracting sounds with soothing background noise.

Setting Boundaries
Creating physical and psychological boundaries is crucial for those sharing their home with others. Setting clear guidelines on work hours and interruptions can help minimize disruptions. Using visual cues, like a closed door or a "Do Not Disturb" sign, can communicate to others that you are in work mode.

Regular Maintenance and Evolution
A productive workspace is not a set-it-and-forget-it endeavor. Regularly reevaluating and adjusting the setup based on changing needs or new insights can enhance functionality and comfort. This might involve upgrading equipment, reorganizing the layout, or introducing new elements that boost productivity.

Creating and maintaining a productive home workspace is a dynamic process that involves careful consideration of location, ergonomics, organization, personalization, and technology. By crafting an environment that supports focus, comfort, and efficiency, remote workers and home-based entrepreneurs can optimize their productivity and enjoy a fulfilling work-life balance from the comfort of their homes.

Overcoming common work-from-home challenges
Transitioning to a work-from-home setup presents a unique set of challenges that, if not addressed, can impede productivity, well-being, and work-life balance. Recognizing and strategically overcoming these hurdles is crucial for remote workers and home-based entrepreneurs to thrive in their professional and personal lives.

Isolation and Loneliness
One of the most significant challenges of remote work is the potential for isolation and loneliness, given the lack of in-person interaction with colleagues and peers. Overcoming this requires intentional effort to maintain social connections:

Virtual Collaboration: Utilize video conferencing and collaboration tools not just for meetings, but for casual catch-ups and virtual coffee breaks with colleagues.

Online Communities: Engage with online communities and professional networks related to your field to share insights, seek advice, and maintain a sense of belonging.

Co-working Spaces: Occasionally working from co-working spaces or cafes (if feasible) can provide a change of scenery and the opportunity to interact with others.

Distractions and Lack of Focus
The home environment is replete with potential distractions, from household chores to family members, that can derail focus and productivity:

Dedicated Workspace: Establish a dedicated, quiet workspace where distractions are minimized, signaling to both yourself and household members that you are in 'work mode.'
Time Management Techniques: Employ time management techniques like the Pomodoro Technique or time blocking to structure your day and dedicate focused time to tasks.
Clear Boundaries: Set clear boundaries with family and housemates regarding your work hours and space, educating them on the importance of minimizing interruptions.
Blurring of Work-Life Boundaries

Without the physical separation of an office, distinguishing between work and personal time can become challenging, often leading to overwork or the inability to disconnect:

Structured Schedule: Maintain a structured daily schedule with defined start and end times to your workday, including regular breaks.

Physical and Digital Boundaries: Physically step away from your workspace during breaks and after hours, and use digital tools to mute work notifications outside of work hours.

Mindful Transitions: Create rituals that mark the beginning and end of the workday, such as a morning walk before starting or a specific activity to signal the end of work, helping to mentally transition between work and personal time.

Maintaining Motivation and Accountability

Without the immediate presence of supervisors and colleagues, maintaining a high level of motivation and accountability can be challenging:

Set Clear Goals: Establish clear, achievable goals and track your progress to maintain direction and motivation.

Accountability Partners: Partner with a colleague, mentor, or coach with whom you can share progress, challenges, and successes, creating a sense of accountability.

Celebrate Milestones: Recognize and celebrate achievements, no matter how small, to maintain motivation and a sense of accomplishment.

Managing Workload and Avoiding Burnout

The flexibility of remote work can sometimes lead to taking on too much work, resulting in stress and potential burnout:

Prioritize Tasks: Use prioritization methods to focus on high-impact tasks, ensuring that your energy is directed toward work that advances your goals.

<u>Learn to Say No</u>: Develop the ability to decline additional responsibilities when your workload is full, protecting your time and well-being.

<u>Self-Care:</u> Integrate self-care practices into your daily routine, including exercise, hobbies, and relaxation techniques, to maintain mental and physical health.

Technical Issues and Connectivity

Reliance on technology means that technical issues and connectivity problems can significantly disrupt work:

<u>Reliable Internet Connection:</u> Invest in a reliable internet service and consider a backup option, such as a mobile hotspot, to ensure continuous connectivity.

<u>Tech Support:</u> Have a plan for tech support, whether it's through professional services or becoming familiar with basic troubleshooting for your key devices and software.

Overcoming the challenges of working from home involves a combination of creating structured routines, leveraging technology, maintaining social connections, and setting boundaries. By proactively addressing these common hurdles, remote workers and home-based entrepreneurs can create a productive, fulfilling, and balanced work-from-home experience.

Chapter 5: Balance or Bust

Strategies for maintaining work-life balance

Achieving a harmonious work-life balance is a crucial aspect of remote work, pivotal for ensuring long-term well-being, productivity, and personal fulfillment. The flexibility of working from home offers unique opportunities to blend professional and personal life seamlessly, yet it also poses challenges in drawing clear boundaries. Implementing strategic practices can help remote workers and home-based entrepreneurs navigate these challenges, fostering a balanced and rewarding lifestyle.

Set Clear Work Hours

Defining specific work hours is essential in establishing a routine that separates work from personal time. Stick to these hours as consistently as possible, and communicate them to colleagues and household members to set expectations. This structure mimics the traditional office environment, providing a psychological cue that helps in switching between professional and personal modes.

Designate a Dedicated Workspace

Having a physical space designated solely for work can significantly enhance the separation between professional duties and home life. This space should be equipped with all necessary work-related items, minimizing the need to move around the house and blurring lines between work and leisure areas. At the end of the workday, physically leaving this space can signal the brain that work has concluded, aiding in the mental transition to personal time.

Leverage Technology Wisely

While technology is a boon for productivity and connectivity, it can also tether workers to their jobs beyond work hours. Use technology settings to your advantage by turning off work-related notifications after hours and during weekends. Employ apps that promote focus and limit distractions during work hours, ensuring productivity within the designated work time.

Prioritize Tasks and Delegate

Understanding that not every task holds equal weight is crucial in managing workload effectively. Prioritize tasks based on urgency and importance, focusing on those that significantly impact your goals. Learn to delegate tasks when possible, whether within a professional context or by sharing household responsibilities, to prevent overextension and burnout.

Incorporate Breaks and Downtime

Regular breaks throughout the workday are vital for mental and physical rejuvenation, aiding in sustained productivity. Additionally, ensure that personal time includes activities that relax and recharge you, such as hobbies, exercise, or spending time with loved ones. Downtime is not wasted time but a crucial element in maintaining overall health and well-being.

Stay Physically Active

Integrating physical activity into daily routines is not only beneficial for physical health but also for mental clarity and stress reduction. Whether it's a morning workout, a midday walk, or an evening yoga session, regular exercise can provide a much-needed break from work and contribute to a more balanced lifestyle.

Nurture Social Connections

Maintaining social connections is essential for emotional well-being, particularly for remote workers who may experience feelings of isolation. Make conscious efforts to connect with friends, family, and colleagues through social activities, whether virtually or in person, ensuring these interactions are part of your regular schedule.

Practice Mindfulness and Stress-Reduction Techniques
Mindfulness practices, such as meditation, deep-breathing exercises, or journaling, can help in managing stress and maintaining a clear distinction between work and personal life. These techniques can aid in staying present and grounded, reducing the likelihood of work concerns encroaching on personal time.

Regularly Assess and Adjust
Work-life balance is not a one-size-fits-all formula and can change based on workloads, personal commitments, and life stages. Regularly assess your work-life balance, reflecting on what is working and what isn't. Be open to making adjustments, whether it's changing work hours, tweaking routines, or seeking support to manage responsibilities.

Set Boundaries and Learn to Say No
Setting boundaries is crucial in protecting personal time and energy. This might involve declining work requests that fall outside your work hours, setting expectations with clients, or learning to say no to commitments that do not align with your priorities. Clear boundaries help in managing demands from various aspects of life, preserving time and energy for what truly matters.

Maintaining work-life balance as a remote worker or home-based entrepreneur requires intentional effort and ongoing adjustment. By setting clear boundaries, prioritizing well-being, and staying connected with personal values, individuals can cultivate a fulfilling professional and personal life, even in the fluid environment of home-based work.

The importance of setting boundaries

In the realm of remote work and home-based entrepreneurship, setting boundaries is not just a practice but a necessity. It is the art of drawing lines that separate professional responsibilities from personal life, ensuring neither encroaches undesirably upon the other. The importance of setting boundaries lies in its profound impact on productivity, mental health, and overall work-life harmony.

Defining Professional Boundaries

Professional boundaries delineate the scope of work responsibilities, interactions with colleagues and clients, and the use of time and resources. They help in managing expectations and fostering a professional environment, even within the home setting.

Work Hours: Clearly defined work hours signal to both oneself and others when one is available for professional engagements and when one is off the clock. Adhering to these hours helps in avoiding burnout and ensures time is allocated for rest and personal pursuits.
Communication Guidelines: Establishing guidelines for communication, such as response times, preferred channels, and protocols for urgent matters, can prevent the constant barrage of messages and calls from disrupting work focus and personal time.
Task Prioritization: Setting boundaries around which tasks warrant immediate attention versus those that can wait plays a crucial role in managing workload and stress. It aids in focusing on what truly matters, enhancing efficiency and effectiveness.
Personal Boundaries for Self-Care

Personal boundaries are essential for safeguarding one's well-being, ensuring that time is reserved for self-care, hobbies, and relationships. These boundaries are crucial for mental and emotional health, preventing work from consuming all aspects of life.

Unplugging: Deliberately disconnecting from work-related devices and platforms during personal time helps in mentally and emotionally detaching from work, allowing for genuine relaxation and rejuvenation.

Leisure and Social Activities: Setting boundaries to protect time for leisure and social activities is vital for maintaining a balanced and fulfilling life. It ensures that work does not overshadow the joys and connections that enrich one's life.

Self-Care Practices: Prioritizing self-care practices, whether it's exercise, meditation, or simply quiet reading time, is a boundary that promotes well-being. It signals the importance of health and happiness, independent of professional achievements.

Physical Boundaries Within the Home

In a home-based work setting, physical boundaries are tangible demarcations that separate the workspace from the living space, reinforcing the distinction between 'work time' and 'personal time.'

Dedicated Workspace: Having a designated area for work helps in mentally transitioning into and out of work mode, enhancing focus during work hours and allowing for detachment after hours.

Workspace Organization: Keeping the workspace organized and free from personal clutter reinforces its professional nature, minimizing distractions and maintaining productivity.

Emotional and Mental Boundaries

Emotional and mental boundaries involve safeguarding one's emotional energy and mental space from the demands and stresses of work.

Managing Workload: Recognizing personal limits and communicating them effectively can prevent taking on more work than can be reasonably managed, protecting against stress and burnout.

Emotional Detachment: Cultivating the ability to detach emotionally from work-related stresses after hours is crucial for preserving mental health and ensuring that professional challenges do not unduly affect personal well-being.

Navigating Boundaries with Others

Setting boundaries with household members, colleagues, and clients is crucial in a remote work setting, requiring clear communication and mutual respect.

Household Expectations: Communicating work hours and expectations to household members helps in minimizing interruptions and ensures support for one's work routine.

Professional Interactions: Establishing clear boundaries in professional interactions, such as availability for meetings and expected turnaround times for tasks, helps in managing workload and maintaining professional relationships.

The act of setting and respecting boundaries in a work-from-home context is a dynamic process that requires continuous attention and adjustment. It is about finding the right balance that allows for professional growth and productivity while ensuring personal well-being and fulfillment. By effectively setting boundaries, remote workers and home-based entrepreneurs can navigate the complexities of blending work and life under one roof, fostering an environment where both can thrive.

Incorporating self-care into your routine

In the bustling life of a remote worker or home-based entrepreneur, self-care often takes a backseat to pressing deadlines and professional commitments. However, neglecting self-care can lead to burnout, decreased productivity, and a decline in physical and mental health. Incorporating self-care into daily routines is not just beneficial; it's essential for sustaining long-term success and well-being.

Understanding Self-Care

Self-care encompasses a wide range of practices aimed at maintaining and improving one's health, well-being, and happiness. It involves actively taking steps to care for oneself in four key areas: physical, emotional, mental, and spiritual.

Physical Self-Care: Involves activities that improve physical health, such as exercise, nutrition, sleep, and relaxation techniques.
Emotional Self-Care: Entails managing stress, fostering positive relationships, and engaging in activities that bring joy and relaxation.
Mental Self-Care: Includes practices that stimulate the mind and reduce mental stress, such as reading, learning new skills, or engaging in hobbies.
Spiritual Self-Care: Can involve meditation, spending time in nature, or any activity that helps you connect with a larger purpose or sense of peace.
Integrating Self-Care into Daily Routines

The key to effective self-care is integration into daily life, making it a seamless part of your routine rather than an afterthought.

Scheduled Breaks: Incorporate short breaks throughout the workday for stretching, deep breathing, or a quick walk. These breaks can help reset your energy and improve focus.
Regular Exercise: Schedule regular exercise sessions, whether it's a morning jog, a midday yoga session, or an evening workout. Exercise not only boosts physical health but also improves mood and mental clarity.

Mindful Eating: Take the time to prepare and enjoy nutritious meals, turning mealtime into a break from work and an opportunity to nourish your body.

Quality Sleep: Prioritize getting enough quality sleep, recognizing it as foundational to effective functioning, decision-making, and creativity.

Digital Detox: Set aside time each day or week where you disconnect from all digital devices, allowing your mind to rest and recharge away from screens and notifications.

Emotional Check-ins: Regularly assess your emotional state, acknowledging and addressing feelings of stress, anxiety, or fatigue. Techniques such as journaling or talking with a trusted friend can provide emotional release and perspective.

Learning and Development: Dedicate time to activities that stimulate your mind and contribute to your personal and professional growth, such as reading, online courses, or creative projects.

Mindfulness and Meditation: Incorporate mindfulness practices or meditation into your routine to enhance mental clarity, reduce stress, and improve emotional regulation.

Hobbies and Leisure Activities: Engage in hobbies or activities purely for enjoyment, without any connection to work or productivity. This can include anything from painting and gardening to playing a musical instrument or crafting.

Social Connections: Maintain and nurture relationships with family and friends, recognizing the importance of social support and interaction for emotional well-being.

Creating a Self-Care Plan

Developing a personalized self-care plan involves identifying the activities that most effectively support your well-being and determining how to integrate them into your daily life. This plan should be flexible, allowing for adjustments based on workload, personal commitments, and changing needs.

Assess Needs: Start by assessing your current physical, emotional, mental, and spiritual needs to identify areas that require more attention.

Set Goals: Define specific, achievable self-care goals that address those needs, such as committing to a daily walk, setting a regular bedtime, or practicing meditation.

Plan Activities: Schedule self-care activities, treating them with the same importance as work-related tasks.

Monitor and Adjust: Regularly review your self-care plan, noting what's working and what isn't, and make adjustments as needed.

Incorporating self-care into your routine is not a luxury but a necessity for remote workers and home-based entrepreneurs. By prioritizing self-care, you can enhance your well-being, boost productivity, and enjoy a more fulfilling work-life balance.

Chapter 6: Building Your Brand

Personal branding and its importance for entrepreneurs

In the digital age, where the market is saturated with countless businesses and freelancers, personal branding has emerged as a critical differentiator for entrepreneurs. It's the process of creating and promoting a distinct and consistent image or identity that represents an individual's values, skills, and experiences. For entrepreneurs, particularly those working from home, personal branding is not just about visibility; it's about establishing credibility, building relationships, and communicating the unique value they bring to their industry or niche.

Defining Personal Branding

Personal branding is the deliberate effort to create and influence public perception by positioning an individual as an authority in their industry, elevating their credibility, and differentiating them from the competition. It involves carefully curating aspects of personality, expertise, and values that are communicated through various channels to a targeted audience.

The Importance of Personal Branding for Entrepreneurs

Establishes Credibility and Authority: A strong personal brand showcases an entrepreneur's expertise and knowledge, establishing them as thought leaders in their field. This credibility can attract clients, partners, and opportunities.

Enhances Visibility: In the vast digital landscape, a distinctive personal brand helps entrepreneurs stand out, making it easier for potential clients or customers to discover and remember them.

Builds Trust: People prefer to do business with individuals they know, like, and trust. Personal branding allows entrepreneurs to share their stories, values, and passions, fostering a sense of connection and trust with their audience.

<u>Facilitates Networking</u>: A well-established personal brand opens doors to networking opportunities, collaborations, and partnerships. It makes the individual more approachable and sought after within professional circles.

<u>Drives Business Growth</u>: Ultimately, a strong personal brand can lead to increased business opportunities. It can attract more leads, enable premium pricing based on perceived value, and lead to more referrals and repeat business.

Key Elements of Personal Branding

<u>Authenticity</u>: The foundation of a compelling personal brand is authenticity. It should be a true reflection of the entrepreneur's personality, beliefs, and values, ensuring consistency in how they present themselves online and offline.

<u>Value Proposition</u>: Clearly articulating what makes them unique and how they add value to their clients or customers is crucial. This involves identifying their unique selling points and weaving them into their branding narrative.

<u>Consistency</u>: Consistency in messaging, visual branding, and content across all platforms reinforces brand recognition and reinforces the entrepreneur's professional image.

<u>Visibility</u>: Building a personal brand requires visibility. Regularly sharing content, engaging with the audience, and being active on platforms where the target audience spends time are key strategies.

<u>Networking and Collaboration:</u> Building relationships with other professionals, industry influencers, and potential clients is an integral part of personal branding. Networking, both online and offline, can amplify brand reach and impact.

Strategies for Building a Personal Brand

<u>Define Your Brand Identity:</u> Start by defining the core aspects of your brand—your values, passions, strengths, and the unique perspective you bring to your field.

<u>Create Valuable Content:</u> Share your knowledge, insights, and experiences through blogs, videos, podcasts, or social media posts. Content that provides value to your audience establishes your authority and expertise.

<u>Engage with Your Audience:</u> Interact with your audience through comments, messages, and social media engagements. Listening to their needs and feedback helps build relationships and community.

<u>Leverage Social Media:</u> Use social media platforms strategically to showcase your expertise, share your content, and connect with your audience and peers.

<u>Network and Collaborate:</u> Attend industry events, join professional groups, and seek opportunities for collaboration to expand your network and visibility.

Personal branding for entrepreneurs is an ongoing journey of defining, articulating, and communicating one's unique value and identity in the marketplace. It's about connecting with your audience on a personal level, establishing trust, and positioning yourself as a go-to expert in your field. In the competitive landscape of entrepreneurship, a strong personal brand can be the key to unlocking opportunities, fostering growth, and building a sustainable business.

Utilizing social media and digital marketing

In the digital era, social media and digital marketing have become indispensable tools for entrepreneurs, especially those operating from home. These platforms offer unprecedented opportunities to reach a global audience, engage with potential customers, and build a brand online. Mastering the art of digital marketing allows entrepreneurs to navigate the digital landscape effectively, turning virtual connections into real-world success.

Understanding the Digital Marketing Landscape

Digital marketing encompasses a broad spectrum of activities aimed at promoting businesses, products, or services online. It includes content marketing, search engine optimization (SEO), pay-per-click advertising (PPC), email marketing, and, crucially, social media marketing. Each of these components plays a vital role in a comprehensive digital marketing strategy, offering different advantages and targeting capabilities.

The Power of Social Media

Social media platforms like Facebook, Instagram, Twitter, LinkedIn, and Pinterest have transformed the way businesses connect with their audience. These platforms are not just channels for broadcasting content; they are forums for interaction, engagement, and community building. For home-based entrepreneurs, social media can be a cost-effective way to:

Increase Brand Visibility: Regular posting and engagement can increase your brand's visibility, keeping you top of mind with your audience.

Build Relationships: Social media offers a unique opportunity to build personal relationships with your audience through direct interactions, comments, and messages.

Market Research: Social platforms provide valuable insights into audience preferences, behaviors, and trends, informing product development and marketing strategies.

Drive Traffic: By sharing valuable content, entrepreneurs can drive traffic to their websites or online stores, facilitating lead generation and conversions.

Content Marketing: The Heart of Digital Strategy

Content marketing is about creating and sharing valuable, relevant, and consistent content to attract and retain a clearly defined audience — ultimately, to drive profitable customer action.

For entrepreneurs, content can include blog posts, videos, podcasts, infographics, or ebooks. The key is to provide value, whether through informative, educational, or entertaining content, establishing authority and trust in your niche.

SEO: Enhancing Online Visibility

SEO involves optimizing your website and content to rank higher in search engine results for relevant keywords. This organic visibility is crucial for attracting traffic to your site without the direct cost of advertising. For home-based businesses, local SEO can be particularly effective, targeting potential customers in your geographical area.

Email Marketing: Cultivating Customer Relationships

Email marketing remains one of the most effective digital marketing strategies. It allows for direct communication with your audience, offering personalized content, promotions, and updates. Building a robust email list and delivering regular, valuable emails can foster loyalty and encourage repeat business.

Paid Advertising: Boosting Reach and Engagement

PPC advertising, through platforms like Google AdWords or Facebook Ads, offers a way to reach a broader audience quickly. These ads can be highly targeted based on demographics, interests, and behaviors, ensuring that your marketing messages reach those most likely to be interested in your offerings.

Analyzing and Adapting

One of the greatest advantages of digital marketing is the ability to track and analyze the performance of your campaigns in real-time. Tools like Google Analytics, social media insights, and email marketing software provide valuable data on user behavior, engagement, and conversion rates. Regular analysis of this data allows entrepreneurs to adapt their strategies, optimizing for better results.

Integrating Digital Marketing Efforts

For maximum impact, an entrepreneur's digital marketing efforts should be integrated and cohesive. This means ensuring that messaging is consistent across platforms, campaigns are aligned with overall business goals, and different marketing channels complement and reinforce each other.

Utilizing social media and digital marketing effectively requires a strategic approach, creativity, and adaptability. For home-based entrepreneurs, mastering these digital tools can open up vast opportunities for brand building, audience engagement, and business growth. By leveraging the power of digital marketing, entrepreneurs can not only survive but thrive in the competitive online marketplace.

Networking and community building online

For home-based entrepreneurs and remote workers, the digital realm offers a fertile ground for networking and community building, essential components for business growth and personal development. In an era where physical meetings and traditional networking events are often supplemented or replaced by online interactions, mastering the art of virtual networking becomes crucial. This chapter delves into strategies for cultivating meaningful connections and fostering a supportive community in the digital space.

Leveraging Social Media Platforms

Social media is more than just a marketing tool; it's a networking powerhouse. Platforms like LinkedIn, Twitter, Facebook, and industry-specific forums provide opportunities to connect with peers, mentors, industry leaders, and potential clients.

<u>Active Participation:</u> Regularly engage with content relevant to your field by commenting, sharing, and posting. This visibility can lead to direct interactions with others in your industry.
Joining Groups and Communities: Many social platforms host niche groups or communities where like-minded professionals gather to share insights, ask questions, and support each other. Actively participating in these groups can lead to valuable connections.
<u>Connecting Personally:</u> When you identify potential connections, reach out with personalized messages that reference specific interests or mutual connections. Genuine, personalized engagement can open the door to more meaningful relationships.
Content Creation and Sharing

Sharing original content or insightful commentary on industry trends can position you as a thought leader and attract a network of professionals interested in your expertise.

<u>Blogging:</u> A well-maintained blog can attract readers interested in your field, encouraging professional discussions and connections.
Guest Posting and Collaborations: Contributing to other blogs or collaborating on content can expand your reach and introduce you to the host's network.
Webinars and Online Workshops: Hosting or participating in webinars and workshops not only showcases your expertise but also allows for real-time interaction with a wider audience.

Virtual Networking Events

With the rise of remote work, virtual networking events, conferences, and meetups have become increasingly common. These events can mimic the networking opportunities of in-person events without geographical constraints.

Preparation: Before attending a virtual event, research the speakers, attendees, and topics to identify individuals you'd like to connect with.
Active Engagement: During the event, participate actively by asking questions, contributing to discussions, and following up on interesting points.
Follow-Up: After the event, reach out to individuals you connected with, referencing specific discussions or topics from the event to continue the conversation.

Building and Nurturing an Online Community

Creating or nurturing an online community around your brand or industry can enhance your network and establish you as a central figure in your niche.

Create a Forum or Group: Platforms like Facebook, LinkedIn, or dedicated forum sites can host your community. Regularly post engaging content, encourage discussions, and facilitate connections among members.
Consistency and Value: Offer consistent value to your community through tips, insights, Q&A sessions, or community highlights. The goal is to create an environment where members feel supported and valued.
Encourage Peer-to-Peer Interaction: Foster an environment where community members can network among themselves, share opportunities, and collaborate, enhancing the overall value of the community.

Personalizing Digital Interactions

Despite the virtual nature of online networking, personalization remains key in building meaningful connections.

<u>Personalized Messages</u>: When reaching out to new connections or responding to comments, personalize your messages to reflect genuine interest and engagement.
<u>Virtual Coffee Chats:</u> Propose one-on-one video calls to deepen connections, discuss mutual interests, or explore potential collaborations in a more personal setting.

Continuous Engagement and Follow-Up

Building a network online is an ongoing process. Regularly engaging with your connections, offering help, sharing relevant opportunities, and keeping in touch through direct messages or emails can strengthen these relationships over time.

Networking and community building online require a strategic approach, consistent engagement, and a genuine interest in fostering relationships. By leveraging digital platforms to connect, share knowledge, and support others, home-based entrepreneurs can cultivate a robust network and vibrant community, crucial for personal growth and business success in the digital age.

Chapter 7: Growth and Scalability

Scaling your business from home

Scaling a business from home involves expanding its capacity, reach, and revenue while managing costs and maintaining quality. For home-based entrepreneurs, this growth must be navigated within the unique constraints and advantages of the home environment. Strategic planning, leveraging technology, and optimizing resources are key to successfully scaling without compromising the flexibility and personal touch that often characterize home-based businesses.

Strategic Planning and Goal Setting

Effective scaling begins with a clear vision and strategic plan. Define what scaling means for your business—whether it's reaching new markets, increasing product lines, or boosting production capacity. Set specific, measurable goals aligned with this vision, and outline the steps required to achieve them.

Market Analysis: Conduct thorough market research to identify new opportunities for growth, understand customer needs, and anticipate market trends.

Financial Planning: Assess the financial implications of scaling, including the need for investment, cash flow management, and profitability forecasts. A solid financial plan will guide decision-making and investment priorities.

Leveraging Technology and Automation

Technology can be a great enabler for scaling businesses from home, allowing for more efficient operations, wider reach, and better customer engagement.

Automation Tools: Implement tools that automate repetitive tasks, such as email marketing, customer service responses, and invoicing. This frees up time to focus on strategic growth activities.
E-commerce Platforms: Utilize robust e-commerce platforms to expand your online presence, streamline sales processes, and manage inventory more effectively.
Cloud-Based Solutions: Adopt cloud-based services for collaboration, project management, and data storage, facilitating seamless remote work and scalability.

Outsourcing and Delegation

As the business grows, it becomes crucial to delegate tasks and possibly outsource certain functions to manage workload and maintain focus on core growth activities.

Identify Core Competencies: Focus on your strengths and core business activities, and consider outsourcing non-core tasks, such as accounting, IT support, or content creation.
Virtual Assistants and Freelancers: Hiring virtual assistants or freelancers can provide flexible support for administrative tasks, marketing, or other specialized areas without the need for full-time employees.

Building a Scalable Business Model

Your business model must be capable of accommodating growth without proportional increases in costs or resources.

Passive Income Streams: Develop passive income streams, such as digital products, subscription services, or affiliate marketing, that can scale without constant input.
Scalable Product Lines: Design products or services that are easily scalable, considering factors like production, delivery, and customer support at larger volumes.

Customer Experience and Retention

Maintaining high-quality customer service and a personalized experience is vital during scaling, ensuring customer satisfaction and loyalty.

Customer Relationship Management (CRM) Systems: Implement CRM systems to manage customer interactions, personalize communication, and ensure consistent service quality.
Feedback Loops: Establish mechanisms for regular customer feedback to continuously improve products and services and address any issues promptly.

Expanding Market Reach

Growth often involves reaching new customers and markets, requiring targeted marketing strategies and possibly localization of products or services.

Digital Marketing: Enhance digital marketing efforts to reach a broader audience, using SEO, content marketing, and social media strategies.
Market Diversification: Explore new market segments or geographical areas where your products or services could meet unfulfilled needs.

Maintaining Operational Efficiency
As operations expand, maintaining efficiency becomes more challenging but increasingly important.

Process Optimization: Regularly review and optimize operational processes to eliminate inefficiencies and streamline workflows.
Quality Control: Implement quality control measures to ensure that product or service quality remains high as volume increases.

Scaling a business from home requires a delicate balance between growth and sustainability.

It involves careful planning, leveraging technology, and optimizing operations, all while maintaining the essence and personal touch that often defines home-based businesses. With the right strategies in place, entrepreneurs can successfully expand their ventures, reaching new heights of success from the comfort of their homes.

Outsourcing and automation for efficiency

For home-based entrepreneurs, the twin strategies of outsourcing and automation represent powerful tools for enhancing efficiency, managing workload, and focusing on core business activities. As businesses grow, the demands on time and resources increase, making it crucial to find effective ways to streamline operations. Outsourcing tasks to external professionals and automating repetitive processes can significantly boost productivity, allowing entrepreneurs to scale their operations more effectively.

The Role of Outsourcing

Outsourcing involves delegating specific tasks or functions to third-party providers or freelancers. This strategy can be particularly beneficial for tasks that are outside an entrepreneur's area of expertise or for activities that are time-consuming but not directly related to generating revenue.

Identifying Tasks for Outsourcing: The first step in effective outsourcing is to identify tasks that can be delegated. These might include administrative duties, content creation, graphic design, accounting, or IT support. The key is to focus on tasks that are necessary but not necessarily the best use of the entrepreneur's time.

Choosing the Right Partners: Selecting the right vendors, freelancers, or agencies is crucial. Look for providers with a proven track record, positive reviews, and clear communication channels. It's also important to ensure that their values and work ethic align with your business goals.

<u>Managing Outsourced Work:</u> Effective communication and clear expectations are essential for successful outsourcing. This includes setting clear deadlines, providing detailed briefs, and establishing regular check-ins to ensure alignment and quality control.

Leveraging Automation

Automation involves using technology to perform repetitive tasks without human intervention. Many aspects of business operations can be automated, from customer communications to billing and social media posting, freeing up valuable time for strategic thinking and core business activities.

<u>Identifying Opportunities for Automation:</u> Review your daily and weekly tasks to identify repetitive processes that can be automated. This might include email responses, social media posting, invoicing, or data entry.

<u>Choosing Automation Tools:</u> There are numerous tools available for automating different aspects of business operations. For example, email marketing can be automated with tools like Mailchimp or Constant Contact, while social media management can be streamlined using platforms like Hootsuite or Buffer.

<u>Implementing and Monitoring Automation:</u> Once suitable tools have been selected, the next step is implementation. This might involve setting up automated workflows, creating content in advance, or programming software to perform specific tasks. Regular monitoring is essential to ensure that automated processes are functioning correctly and to make adjustments as necessary.

Benefits of Outsourcing and Automation

Increased Focus on Core Activities: By delegating non-core tasks and automating repetitive processes, entrepreneurs can devote more time and energy to strategic planning, business development, and other high-value activities.
Scalability: Outsourcing and automation make it easier to scale operations by adding resources or increasing activity without a corresponding increase in workload or staffing.
Cost Efficiency: Outsourcing can be more cost-effective than hiring full-time staff for specific tasks, especially for specialized skills or fluctuating workloads. Automation can reduce the time spent on routine tasks, lowering operational costs.
Flexibility: Both outsourcing and automation offer flexibility, allowing businesses to adapt quickly to changing demands or market conditions without the need for significant restructuring.

Challenges and Considerations

While outsourcing and automation offer numerous benefits, they also come with challenges. It's important to maintain quality control when outsourcing and to ensure that automated processes do not compromise the personal touch or customer service quality. Clear communication, regular reviews, and a strategic approach are essential to navigate these challenges effectively.

Outsourcing and automation are key strategies for home-based entrepreneurs looking to enhance efficiency and productivity. By carefully selecting tasks for delegation and implementing automation where appropriate, entrepreneurs can streamline operations, focus on growth, and build a more sustainable and scalable business from the comfort of their home.

Diversification of income streams

In the volatile landscape of entrepreneurship, particularly for those operating from home, diversifying income streams can provide stability, reduce risk, and open up new avenues for growth. This chapter explores the concept of income diversification, why it's essential for home-based businesses, and practical ways to implement it.

Understanding Income Diversification

Income diversification involves creating multiple revenue sources, so the business isn't reliant on a single product, service, or client. This strategy not only cushions the business against market fluctuations but also capitalizes on new opportunities, enhancing overall financial resilience.

Benefits of Diversifying Income

Risk Mitigation: Diversification spreads financial risk across multiple revenue streams, ensuring that the underperformance of one area doesn't critically impact the overall business.
Increased Stability: Multiple income sources can provide a more stable and predictable cash flow, crucial for managing operational expenses and planning for growth.
Market Adaptability: Diverse income streams allow businesses to quickly adapt to market changes, consumer trends, or technological advancements, maintaining relevance and competitiveness.
Growth Opportunities: Exploring new products, services, or markets can uncover untapped potential, driving business growth and expansion.

Strategies for Diversifying Income

Expand Product or Service Offerings: Consider broadening your range of products or services to appeal to different customer segments or meet varying needs within your existing market.

Develop Passive Income Streams: Passive income, such as royalties, affiliate marketing, or digital products (e-books, online courses), can generate revenue with minimal ongoing effort after the initial setup.

Offer Subscription Services: Subscription-based models provide recurring revenue and can be applied to various businesses, from content platforms to product delivery services.

Leverage Affiliate Marketing: Earn commissions by promoting other businesses' products or services to your audience. This strategy can be particularly effective if the affiliate offerings are complementary to your own.

Explore Licensing Opportunities: If you have created a unique product or proprietary method, licensing it to other companies can provide a new revenue stream without significant additional workload.

Invest in Other Ventures: With sufficient capital, investing in other businesses, stocks, or real estate can diversify your income sources beyond the operational scope of your primary business.

Implementing Diversification Effectively

Market Research: Before diversifying, conduct thorough market research to understand customer needs, market gaps, and competitive offerings. This ensures that new ventures are viable and align with market demand.

Pilot Projects: Test new products or services on a small scale before full implementation. Pilot projects can provide valuable feedback and indicate potential success without substantial initial investment.

Strategic Partnerships: Collaborate with complementary businesses or entrepreneurs. Partnerships can offer mutual benefits, allowing both parties to tap into new markets or customer bases.

Financial Planning: Careful financial management is crucial when diversifying. Allocate resources wisely, keeping in mind the potential return on investment and the financial sustainability of new ventures.

Continuous Learning: Stay informed about industry trends, technological advancements, and new market opportunities. Ongoing education can inspire innovative ways to diversify your income.

Challenges and Considerations

While diversification offers numerous benefits, it also presents challenges. Spreading resources too thin can dilute focus and impact the quality of your core offerings. It's important to balance the pursuit of new opportunities with the maintenance of your primary business operations.

Furthermore, each new income stream may come with its learning curve, regulatory considerations, and operational requirements. Entrepreneurs must weigh these factors carefully, ensuring they have the capacity and expertise to manage diversification effectively.

Diversifying income streams is a strategic approach to building a resilient, adaptable, and growth-oriented home-based business. By exploring new avenues for revenue, entrepreneurs can safeguard their operations against market uncertainties, capitalize on emerging opportunities, and lay the groundwork for sustained financial success.

Chapter 8: Financial Wisdom for Homepreneurs

Managing finances and maximizing profit

For home-based entrepreneurs, adept financial management is the cornerstone of sustainability and growth. It involves meticulous tracking of income and expenses, strategic pricing, cost control, and profit maximization. This chapter delves into the principles and practices essential for effective financial stewardship, guiding entrepreneurs towards financial health and enhanced profitability in their ventures.

Financial Planning and Budgeting

A robust financial plan serves as a roadmap for your business, outlining expected income, expenses, and profit margins. It helps in setting financial goals and making informed decisions.

Budget Creation: Develop a comprehensive budget that accounts for all potential revenue streams and fixed and variable expenses. This budget should be revisited and adjusted regularly to reflect actual business performance and market changes.

Cash Flow Management: Effective cash flow management ensures that the business has sufficient cash to cover its obligations. This involves careful timing of income and expenditures, maintaining an emergency cash reserve, and managing credit terms with suppliers and customers.

Cost Control and Expense Management

Keeping expenses in check is crucial for maintaining profitability. This doesn't necessarily mean minimizing costs at all costs but rather ensuring that each expense contributes to business value.

<u>Regular Expense Review:</u> Regularly review and categorize expenses to identify areas where costs can be reduced or eliminated without compromising product or service quality.

<u>Invest in Efficiency:</u> Consider investments in technology, tools, or outsourcing that could streamline operations and reduce long-term costs, even if they require upfront expenditure.

Revenue Streams and Pricing Strategies

Diversifying income and setting the right price points for products or services are pivotal in maximizing profitability.

<u>Market-Based Pricing:</u> Pricing should be competitive yet reflective of the value provided. Conduct market research to understand competitor pricing and customer willingness to pay.

<u>Value Proposition:</u> Ensure that your pricing strategy aligns with your value proposition. Customers are often willing to pay a premium for products or services that offer significant value or unique benefits.

<u>Multiple Revenue Streams:</u> As discussed in the previous chapter, diversifying income sources can stabilize and increase revenue, contributing to overall profitability.

Monitoring Financial Performance

Regular monitoring of financial metrics is essential to understand the health of the business and guide strategic decisions.

<u>Key Performance Indicators (KPIs):</u> Identify and track KPIs relevant to your business, such as profit margins, revenue growth, customer acquisition cost, and lifetime value. These indicators provide insights into business performance and areas needing improvement.

<u>Financial Statements:</u> Regularly review financial statements, including the income statement, balance sheet, and cash flow statement, to get a comprehensive view of the financial health of your business.

Tax Planning and Compliance

Understanding and complying with tax obligations is crucial to avoid penalties and optimize tax liabilities.

Tax Planning: Engage in tax planning to take advantage of allowable deductions, credits, and tax-efficient business structures. Consider consulting with a tax professional to ensure compliance and optimize tax strategies.
Keep Accurate Records: Maintain meticulous records of all business transactions, receipts, and expenses for tax purposes. This not only aids in tax preparation but also provides valuable financial data for business analysis.

Investing in Growth

Reinvesting profits back into the business can fuel growth and expansion. Identify areas with the highest return on investment, such as marketing, product development, or market expansion, to allocate resources effectively.

Strategic Reinvestment: Decide on reinvestment strategies based on long-term business goals, market opportunities, and financial stability.
Measure ROI: Continuously assess the return on investment of reinvested funds to ensure they are driving desired growth and profitability.
Effective financial management and profit maximization require a balance between strategic planning, diligent monitoring, and adaptive decision-making. By mastering these financial principles, home-based entrepreneurs can build a strong economic foundation, enabling their businesses to thrive and grow sustainably.

Investment strategies for long-term growth

For entrepreneurs steering their home-based businesses towards long-term growth, adopting sound investment strategies is essential. This involves not just the reinvestment of profits back into the business, but also exploring external investment opportunities to build wealth and secure the future. Balancing risk, understanding market trends, and making informed decisions are key to developing an effective investment portfolio that supports both personal financial goals and the business's expansion ambitions.

Reinvesting in the Business

One of the most immediate forms of investment for home-based entrepreneurs is plowing profits back into the business. This reinvestment can take various forms, each aimed at bolstering the business's growth potential:

Product or Service Development: Investing in the research and development of new products or the enhancement of existing offerings can help in capturing a larger market share and increasing competitiveness.

Market Expansion: Expanding into new geographical areas or demographics requires capital, whether for marketing, logistics, or establishing local partnerships.

Operational Efficiency: Upgrading technology, software, or equipment can streamline operations, improve product quality, and reduce long-term costs, contributing to profitability.

Diversifying Income through External Investments

Beyond reinvesting in the business, entrepreneurs should consider building an external investment portfolio. Diversification across different asset classes can mitigate risk and provide a financial safety net.

<u>Stock Market:</u> Equity investments in publicly traded companies offer the potential for significant returns but come with higher volatility. A mix of stocks, considering different industries and geographical locations, can spread risk.

<u>Bonds:</u> Bonds provide a more stable investment option, offering fixed interest payments over time. Government and corporate bonds are common choices for investors seeking lower-risk options.

<u>Real Estate:</u> Investing in real estate can provide steady income through rental yields and potential capital appreciation. However, it requires significant capital and comes with its own set of risks and responsibilities.

<u>Mutual Funds and ETFs:</u> Mutual funds and exchange-traded funds (ETFs) allow investors to pool their money in a diversified portfolio managed by professionals, reducing the risk associated with individual investments.

Retirement Planning

For entrepreneurs, whose income can often fluctuate, planning for retirement is crucial. Establishing a retirement savings plan can ensure financial security in later years.

<u>Individual Retirement Accounts (IRAs):</u> Traditional or Roth IRAs offer a way to save for retirement with tax advantages. The choice between them depends on current income levels and anticipated post-retirement tax rates.

<u>Self-Employed Pension Plans:</u> Plans like SEP IRAs or Solo 401(k)s are designed for self-employed individuals, offering higher contribution limits and tax benefits.

Risk Management and Asset Allocation

Effective investment strategies involve managing risk through careful asset allocation. This means spreading investments across various asset classes to balance potential returns with risk tolerance.

Risk Assessment: Regularly assess your risk tolerance based on personal financial goals, business stability, and market conditions. This assessment should guide investment decisions and asset allocation.
Portfolio Review: Continuously monitor and adjust your investment portfolio to respond to market changes, personal circumstances, or shifts in financial goals.

Seeking Professional Advice

The complexity of investment strategies and the ever-changing market dynamics often necessitate professional guidance.

Financial Advisors: A qualified financial advisor can provide personalized advice based on your financial situation, risk tolerance, and long-term goals.
Continuous Learning: Stay informed about financial markets, investment tools, and economic trends. Ongoing education is vital for making informed investment decisions.

Investment strategies for long-term growth encompass a broad spectrum of opportunities, from reinvesting in the business to diversifying through external investments. For home-based entrepreneurs, these strategies are not just about immediate returns but building a stable financial foundation that supports both personal and business objectives over the long term. Balancing risk, staying informed, and possibly seeking professional advice are key to navigating the complexities of investment and securing long-term growth and financial stability.

The importance of savings and emergency funds

For entrepreneurs, especially those operating from home, the financial landscape can be unpredictable, marked by fluctuating income streams and unforeseen expenses. In this context, building savings and establishing an emergency fund are not just prudent financial strategies but essential safeguards that ensure business continuity and personal financial security. This chapter explores the critical role of savings and emergency funds in buffering against financial volatility and supporting long-term stability.

Understanding Savings and Emergency Funds

Savings: Savings typically refer to the portion of income set aside for future use, which is not earmarked for immediate expenses or high-risk investments. Savings can serve various purposes, from funding planned expenditures like vacations or home improvements to serving as a financial cushion.

Emergency Fund: An emergency fund is a specific type of savings dedicated to covering unexpected and urgent financial needs, such as medical emergencies, urgent home repairs, or sustaining operations during a sudden loss of income. The key characteristic of an emergency fund is liquidity—funds should be easily accessible without incurring penalties or significant losses.

Benefits of Having an Emergency Fund

Financial Security: An emergency fund provides a sense of security, knowing that you have a financial buffer to fall back on in times of need. This can reduce stress and allow for more focused decision-making in both personal and business matters.

<u>Business Continuity:</u> For home-based businesses, an emergency fund can be the difference between weathering a rough patch and being forced to close. It can cover operational costs during slow periods, ensuring the business stays afloat.

<u>Avoiding Debt:</u> With an emergency fund in place, you can cover unexpected expenses without resorting to high-interest credit cards or loans, which can lead to a cycle of debt.

Building Savings

Set Clear Goals: Define what you're saving for, whether it's a personal goal, a business expansion, or simply the peace of mind that comes with having a financial cushion. Setting clear goals can motivate consistent saving.

<u>Automate Savings:</u> Automating the transfer of a certain portion of income into a savings account can help in building savings without the need to remember to set aside money manually each month.

<u>Monitor and Adjust:</u> Regularly review your savings goals and progress, adjusting your contributions as your financial situation changes or as you reach your goals.

Creating an Emergency Fund

<u>Determine the Size of the Fund:</u> Conventional wisdom suggests that an emergency fund should cover 3-6 months' worth of living expenses and operational business costs. However, the exact amount can vary based on personal circumstances, business model, and risk factors.

<u>Start Small:</u> If building a large emergency fund seems daunting, start small. Even a modest fund can provide some security and can be built up over time.

<u>Keep it Accessible but Separate:</u> Your emergency fund should be kept in an account that allows easy access without penalties or significant delays. However, it should be separate from your

regular checking account to avoid the temptation to dip into it for non-emergencies.

Challenges in Building and Maintaining Funds

<u>Variable Income:</u> For entrepreneurs, especially those with new or small businesses, income can be unpredictable, making consistent saving challenging.

<u>Distinguishing Between Wants and Needs:</u> It can be tempting to use funds earmarked for savings or emergencies for non-essential expenses. Maintaining discipline and a clear distinction between wants and needs is crucial.

Strategies for Overcoming Challenges

<u>Budgeting:</u> A detailed budget that accounts for income, fixed expenses, variable expenses, and savings can help in managing finances more effectively.

<u>Incremental Goals:</u> Setting and achieving incremental savings goals can make the process less daunting and more manageable.

The importance of savings and emergency funds in the financial strategy of home-based entrepreneurs cannot be overstated. These funds not only offer a safety net in times of uncertainty but also empower entrepreneurs to make decisions from a position of strength rather than necessity. Building and maintaining these funds requires discipline, planning, and a commitment to long-term financial health.

Chapter 9: Navigating the Rough Waters

Handling setbacks and failures

In the entrepreneurial journey, especially for those operating businesses from home, setbacks and failures are not just possibilities but inventories that test resilience, adaptability, and perseverance. The way an entrepreneur responds to these challenges can significantly influence their long-term success and personal growth. This chapter delves into strategies for effectively handling setbacks and failures, transforming them into opportunities for learning and improvement.

Acknowledging and Accepting Setbacks

The first step in dealing with setbacks is to acknowledge and accept them without personalizing the failure. It's crucial to understand that setbacks are part of the entrepreneurial process, not reflections of personal worth or ability.

Rational Assessment: Take a step back and assess the situation objectively. Identify the factors that led to the setback, distinguishing between those within your control and external influences.
Emotional Acceptance: Allow yourself to process the emotions associated with the setback—frustration, disappointment, or discouragement—without letting them overwhelm your capacity for rational analysis and action.

Learning from Failures

Every setback or failure carries valuable lessons. The key is to extract these lessons and apply them to future endeavors.

<u>Root Cause Analysis:</u> Conduct a thorough analysis to understand the root causes of the failure. This could involve reviewing business processes, financial decisions, market assumptions, or personal management styles.

<u>Seek Feedback:</u> Engage with mentors, peers, or customers to gain external perspectives on what went wrong. Objective feedback can provide insights that might not be apparent from an internal viewpoint.

Resilience Building

Resilience is the ability to bounce back from setbacks with renewed strength and wisdom. Cultivating resilience involves developing a positive mindset, maintaining perspective, and building emotional strength.

<u>Positive Mindset:</u> Foster a mindset that views failures as temporary and solvable problems rather than insurmountable obstacles. Embrace the philosophy that every failure is a stepping stone to success.

<u>Maintain Perspective:</u> Keep setbacks in perspective by reminding yourself of past successes and the overall journey. This helps in preventing the magnification of current failures.

<u>Support Networks:</u> Lean on your support network of family, friends, and fellow entrepreneurs. Sharing experiences and challenges can provide emotional relief and practical advice.

Strategic Pivoting

Sometimes, setbacks require a strategic pivot or a significant change in direction. This could involve altering the business model, exploring new markets, or revamping products/services.

Flexibility: Be open to changing course if persistent setbacks indicate that the current strategy is not viable. Flexibility and adaptability are key traits of successful entrepreneurs.

Informed Decision-Making: Base pivoting decisions on thorough research and analysis, ensuring that the new direction is grounded in viable market opportunities and business strengths.

Maintaining Momentum

It's essential to keep moving forward, even in the face of setbacks. Maintaining momentum ensures that failures do not halt progress but become integrated into the journey.

Small Wins: Focus on achieving small, manageable wins to rebuild confidence and momentum. These successes can help in regaining a positive outlook and motivation.

Action Planning: Develop a clear action plan that addresses the causes of the setback and outlines steps for recovery and future prevention.

Self-Care and Well-Being

Handling setbacks and failures can be emotionally and physically draining. Prioritizing self-care during these times is crucial for maintaining well-being and ensuring that you have the energy and clarity to address challenges.

Physical Health: Maintain healthy routines involving exercise, nutrition, and sleep. Physical well-being significantly impacts mental and emotional resilience.

Mental Health: Engage in activities that reduce stress and promote mental health, such as meditation, hobbies, or spending time with loved ones.

Handling setbacks and failures effectively is a critical skill for home-based entrepreneurs. By approaching these challenges with a constructive mindset, seeking learning opportunities, building resilience, and maintaining momentum, entrepreneurs can navigate the ups and downs of business with grace and emerge stronger and more prepared for future success.

Adapting to market changes and customer needs

In the fast-paced world of entrepreneurship, especially for those operating from a home base, the ability to swiftly adapt to market changes and evolving customer needs is not just an advantage—it's a necessity for survival and growth. The dynamic nature of today's business environment, fueled by technological advancements, shifting consumer behaviors, and global trends, requires entrepreneurs to be vigilant, flexible, and proactive. This chapter explores strategies for staying ahead of the curve and ensuring your business remains relevant and competitive.

Staying Informed

Keeping abreast of industry trends, market research, and consumer insights is foundational to anticipating changes and adapting effectively.

<u>Continuous Learning:</u> Commit to ongoing education in your field. Attend webinars, subscribe to industry publications, and participate in relevant forums and discussions.

<u>Market Research:</u> Regularly conduct or review market research to understand emerging trends, technologies, and consumer preferences.

<u>Competitive Analysis:</u> Keep an eye on competitors and industry leaders. Their movements can provide early indicators of market shifts or new opportunities.

Engaging with Customers

Your customers are a valuable source of insights and feedback. Engaging with them can provide direct information on changing needs and satisfaction levels.

Customer Feedback Channels: Establish and maintain open channels for customer feedback, such as surveys, social media interactions, and review platforms.

Active Listening: Pay attention to customer comments, complaints, and suggestions. Look for patterns or recurring themes that might indicate broader market trends.

Community Engagement: Build a community around your brand where customers can engage, share experiences, and provide insights. This can be facilitated through social media groups, forums, or loyalty programs.

Building a Flexible Business Model

A flexible business model allows you to pivot or make adjustments in response to market changes without overhauling your entire operation.

Scalable Processes: Design business processes and systems that can scale up or down easily, accommodating changes in demand or operational shifts.

Diversified Offerings: Avoid over-reliance on a single product or service. A diversified portfolio can buffer against market volatility and open up multiple revenue streams.

Innovation Culture: Foster a culture of innovation within your business, encouraging experimentation and the exploration of new ideas and approaches.

Leveraging Technology

Technology can be a powerful enabler in adapting to market changes, allowing for more efficient operations, better customer engagement, and new product or service development.

Digital Tools: Utilize digital tools and platforms for better market analysis, customer relationship management (CRM), and operational efficiency.

E-commerce Adaptation: Ensure your online presence, including e-commerce platforms, is optimized, user-friendly, and up-to-date with the latest digital marketing practices.

Product Innovation: Use technology to innovate your product or service offerings, whether through improved features, digital products, or enhanced customer experiences.

Strategic Partnerships

Collaborating with other businesses or industry partners can provide additional resources, insights, and channels to navigate market changes more effectively.

Collaborative Networks: Build networks with non-competing businesses in your industry. These partnerships can lead to shared insights, joint ventures, or co-marketing initiatives.

Supplier Relationships: Maintain strong relationships with suppliers and service providers. They can be valuable sources of information on industry trends and supply chain innovations.

Risk Management and Contingency Planning

Being prepared for unforeseen market shifts or customer behavior changes involves having a risk management strategy and contingency plans in place.

Scenario Planning: Develop scenarios for potential market changes and outline how your business would respond to each scenario.

Financial Reserves: Maintain financial reserves or a line of credit to ensure you have the capital necessary to pivot or adapt your business operations quickly.

Adapting to market changes and customer needs is an ongoing process that requires attention, agility, and a willingness to evolve.

By staying informed, engaging with customers, leveraging technology, and fostering partnerships, home-based entrepreneurs can not only survive but thrive amidst the constant flux of the business landscape. This proactive and responsive approach ensures that your business remains aligned with market dynamics and customer expectations, driving long-term success and growth.

Maintaining motivation and resilience

For home-based entrepreneurs, the journey is often a solo venture fraught with challenges, fluctuating motivation, and the need for unwavering resilience. The ability to maintain a high level of motivation and resilience is not just beneficial but essential for navigating the ups and downs of entrepreneurship. This chapter delves into strategies and practices that can help entrepreneurs sustain their drive and bounce back from setbacks with greater strength and determination.

Understanding Motivation and Resilience

Motivation: Motivation is the internal drive that propels individuals toward their goals. It can be influenced by a variety of factors, including personal values, interests, and the desire for achievement or recognition.

Resilience: Resilience is the capacity to recover quickly from difficulties. It's about having the mental and emotional toughness to face challenges head-on and emerge stronger on the other side.

Strategies for Sustaining Motivation

Maintaining a constant level of motivation requires intentional effort and self-awareness. Here are some strategies to keep the motivational fire burning:

Set Clear, Achievable Goals: Break down your long-term objectives into smaller, manageable tasks. The sense of achievement from completing these tasks can fuel further motivation.
Find Your 'Why': Keep your underlying motivations in mind. Whether it's financial independence, passion for your product, or the desire to make an impact, reminding yourself of your 'why' can reignite your drive.
Celebrate Milestones: Acknowledge and celebrate each milestone, no matter how small. This recognition can provide a sense of progress and accomplishment.
Maintain Work-Life Balance: Ensure you have time for relaxation and activities you enjoy outside of work. A well-balanced life can prevent burnout and keep motivation levels high.

Building Resilience

Developing resilience is a proactive process that involves strengthening your emotional and mental fortitude. Here are ways to build and maintain resilience:

Embrace Challenges as Opportunities: View each challenge as an opportunity to learn and grow. This mindset shift can transform obstacles into stepping stones.

Develop a Support Network: Build a network of friends, family, and fellow entrepreneurs who can offer support, advice, and a listening ear during tough times.

Practice Self-Care: Regularly engage in activities that promote mental, emotional, and physical well-being. Exercise, meditation, hobbies, and adequate rest are vital for resilience.

Learn from Setbacks: Instead of dwelling on failures, analyze them to extract lessons and strategies for improvement. This approach fosters a growth mindset, essential for resilience.

Maintaining a Positive Outlook

A positive outlook can significantly impact motivation and resilience. Cultivating positivity involves:

Practicing Gratitude: Regularly reflect on and appreciate what you're thankful for. Gratitude can shift focus from challenges to positives, enhancing overall well-being.

Visualizing Success: Regularly visualize achieving your goals. This mental rehearsal can boost confidence and motivation.

Limiting Negative Self-Talk: Be mindful of and challenge negative thoughts or self-doubt. Replace them with positive affirmations and constructive self-dialogue.

Staying Flexible and Adaptable

The ability to adapt to changing circumstances without losing sight of your goals is crucial for maintaining motivation and resilience.

Be Open to Change: Accept that change is a part of the entrepreneurial journey. Being flexible in your plans and strategies can help you navigate unexpected turns.

Continuous Learning: Commit to lifelong learning. Gaining new skills and knowledge can inspire innovation and adaptability, keeping you motivated and resilient.

Seeking Inspiration

Look outside your immediate circle for inspiration. Books, podcasts, TED Talks, and stories of successful entrepreneurs can provide fresh perspectives and motivational boosts.

Maintaining motivation and resilience is a dynamic process that requires continuous attention and nurturing. By implementing these strategies, home-based entrepreneurs can cultivate the inner drive and toughness needed to overcome obstacles, stay focused on their goals, and achieve long-term success in their ventures.

Chapter 10: The Future of Home Hustling

Emerging trends in remote work and entrepreneurship

The landscape of remote work and entrepreneurship is ever-evolving, driven by technological advancements, shifting societal norms, and global economic factors. Staying attuned to emerging trends is crucial for home-based entrepreneurs seeking to adapt, innovate, and remain competitive. This chapter explores current and emerging trends shaping the future of remote work and entrepreneurship, offering insights into how these trends can be leveraged for business growth and sustainability.

Rise of the Digital Nomad Lifestyle

The digital nomad lifestyle, characterized by working remotely while traveling, has gained significant traction. Advances in technology and a growing acceptance of remote work have made this lifestyle more feasible and attractive for a wide range of professionals.

Implications: Entrepreneurs must consider the global nature of business and the importance of flexible, cloud-based systems that support mobility and connectivity from anywhere in the world.
Increased Emphasis on Work-Life Integration

As remote work blurs the lines between personal and professional life, there's a shifting focus from work-life balance to work-life integration, where work and personal activities coexist harmoniously throughout the day.

Implications: Entrepreneurs need to adopt flexible work policies and practices that accommodate diverse working styles and personal commitments, promoting well-being and productivity.

Advancements in Remote Collaboration Technologies

The demand for effective remote collaboration tools continues to rise, leading to rapid advancements in communication and project management technologies.

Implications: Staying updated on and integrating the latest collaboration tools can enhance team efficiency, foster innovation, and improve client engagement in a remote setting.
Growing Importance of Online Presence and Digital Marketing

In an increasingly digital world, a strong online presence and savvy digital marketing strategies have become essential for reaching and engaging target audiences.

Implications: Entrepreneurs must invest in building a robust online brand, leveraging social media, SEO, and content marketing to attract and retain customers.
Shift Towards Freelance and Gig Economy

The gig economy is expanding, with more professionals seeking freelance opportunities for flexibility and autonomy. This trend is changing the traditional employment landscape and how businesses source talent.

Implications: Entrepreneurs can tap into a global talent pool for project-based work, enabling scalability and access to diverse skill sets without the commitment of full-time hiring.
Sustainability and Social Responsibility

Consumers are increasingly favoring businesses that demonstrate sustainability and social responsibility. Environmental impact, ethical practices, and community engagement are becoming significant factors in consumer decision-making.

<u>Implications:</u> Incorporating sustainable practices and social responsibility into business models can enhance brand reputation, customer loyalty, and competitive advantage.

AI and Automation in Business Operations

Artificial intelligence (AI) and automation are transforming business operations, offering new opportunities for efficiency, personalization, and innovation.

<u>Implications:</u> Entrepreneurs should explore AI and automation solutions to streamline operations, enhance customer experiences, and unlock new business opportunities.

Rising Focus on Mental Health and Well-Being

The mental health and well-being of entrepreneurs and their teams are gaining attention as critical components of business success and sustainability.

<u>Implications:</u> Implementing practices and policies that support mental health, such as flexible schedules, wellness programs, and open dialogues about mental well-being, can contribute to a healthier, more productive work environment.

Customization and Personalization

The demand for customized and personalized products and services is increasing, driven by consumer desires for uniqueness and tailored experiences.

<u>Implications:</u> Entrepreneurs should consider how to offer personalized options in their product or service offerings, utilizing data analytics and customer feedback to meet individual preferences and needs.

Staying abreast of these emerging trends in remote work and entrepreneurship allows home-based business owners to strategically position themselves for success in a rapidly changing environment. By embracing innovation, prioritizing flexibility and well-being, and committing to continuous learning and adaptation, entrepreneurs can navigate the challenges and opportunities of the modern business landscape, driving long-term growth and resilience.

Preparing for the future of work

As the landscape of work undergoes profound transformations driven by technological advancements, globalization, and changing societal values, home-based entrepreneurs and remote workers face both unprecedented challenges and opportunities. Preparing for the future of work requires not only adaptability and foresight but also a proactive approach to embracing new paradigms and leveraging emerging trends. This chapter explores key strategies and considerations for navigating the evolving work environment, ensuring that businesses and individuals remain resilient, competitive, and future-ready.

Embracing Lifelong Learning

The rapid pace of technological change necessitates a commitment to continuous learning and skill development. Staying updated with industry trends, emerging technologies, and new business practices is crucial for maintaining relevance and competitive edge.

<u>Online Education and Training</u>: Leverage online platforms offering courses, certifications, and workshops in your field, as well as in areas of emerging technology and business innovation.

<u>Cross-disciplinary Skills</u>: Cultivate a diverse skill set that spans beyond your primary area of expertise, including digital literacy, data analysis, and soft skills like critical thinking and communication.

Leveraging Technology and Innovation

Technology is a key driver of change in the future of work, offering tools to enhance productivity, creativity, and connectivity. Embracing technological advancements can streamline operations, open new channels for customer engagement, and create novel business opportunities.

<u>Automation and AI:</u> Explore automation tools and AI-driven solutions to optimize business processes, from customer service chatbots to automated marketing and analytics.
<u>Remote Collaboration Tools:</u> Invest in state-of-the-art collaboration platforms that facilitate seamless communication, project management, and teamwork across geographies.
Adopting Flexible Work Models

The traditional 9-to-5 workday is increasingly giving way to more flexible, outcome-based models. Embracing flexibility can attract talent, improve job satisfaction, and drive productivity.

<u>Remote and Hybrid Teams:</u> Be open to remote and hybrid work arrangements, providing the necessary tools and fostering a culture of trust and accountability.
<u>Project-based Work:</u> Consider project-based engagements and the gig economy as means to access specialized skills and scale operations dynamically in response to business needs.

Fostering a Culture of Innovation

A culture that encourages experimentation, creativity, and innovation is essential for adapting to the future of work. Such a culture can propel businesses forward, enabling them to respond to changes and capitalize on new opportunities.

Encourage Experimentation: Create an environment where new ideas and trial-and-error are encouraged, even if they sometimes lead to failure.

Collaborative Ideation: Utilize collaborative platforms and techniques like brainstorming sessions, hackathons, or innovation labs to generate and refine ideas.

Prioritizing Sustainability and Social Responsibility

Sustainability and social responsibility are becoming increasingly important to consumers, employees, and stakeholders. Integrating these values into your business practices can enhance brand loyalty, attract talent, and contribute to long-term success.

Sustainable Practices: Implement environmentally friendly practices, from reducing waste and energy consumption to sourcing sustainable materials.

Community Engagement: Engage in community service, philanthropy, or social entrepreneurship initiatives that align with your business values and contribute to societal well-being.

Building Resilience and Agility

The ability to quickly adapt to changes and bounce back from setbacks is more crucial than ever. Building resilience and agility within your business operations and workforce can prepare you for unforeseen challenges and volatile market conditions.

Scenario Planning: Regularly engage in scenario planning to anticipate potential challenges and develop contingency plans.

Agile Methodologies: Adopt agile methodologies that allow for rapid iteration and adaptation in product development, marketing strategies, and business operations.

Cultivating a Global Mindset

As businesses become increasingly global, understanding diverse markets, cultures, and regulatory environments is key to expanding reach and tapping into new opportunities.

<u>Cultural Competence:</u> Develop cultural competence within your team to enhance communication, collaboration, and customer relations across diverse geographies.
<u>Global Networks:</u> Build and maintain a global professional network that can provide insights, advice, and partnerships in international markets.

Preparing for the future of work entails a holistic approach that encompasses skill development, technological adoption, flexibility, innovation, sustainability, resilience, and global awareness. For home-based entrepreneurs and remote workers, staying proactive, adaptable, and aligned with emerging trends and values is essential for thriving in the dynamic and evolving work landscape of tomorrow.

Final words of encouragement and empowerment

As we draw near the end of this comprehensive exploration into the multifaceted world of remote work and home-based entrepreneurship, it's crucial to reflect on the journey ahead. The path of an entrepreneur is seldom linear or free from obstacles. Yet, it's these very challenges that mold resilience, foster innovation, and ultimately pave the way to success. This chapter is dedicated to offering words of encouragement and empowerment, aiming to inspire you to embrace the journey with optimism, courage, and an unwavering commitment to your vision.

Embrace the Journey

Entrepreneurship is as much about the journey as it is about the destination. Each step, whether forward or backward, is a part of your unique entrepreneurial story. Embrace every experience, from the triumphs to the setbacks, as an integral piece of the mosaic that constitutes your business journey. Remember, the most profound growth often arises from the most challenging times.

Cultivate Resilience

Resilience is your most valuable asset. It's the force that propels you forward through uncertainty, rejection, and failure. Cultivating resilience involves maintaining a positive outlook, learning from every experience, and viewing setbacks as temporary hurdles rather than insurmountable barriers. Your ability to bounce back and persist in the face of adversity will define your entrepreneurial journey.

Stay Adaptable

In the ever-evolving landscape of business, adaptability is key. Stay open to new ideas, be willing to pivot when necessary, and remain flexible in your strategies and plans. The most successful entrepreneurs are those who can navigate change with agility, seizing opportunities where others see obstacles.

Never Stop Learning

The pursuit of knowledge is endless. In an age where information is at our fingertips, the potential for learning and growth is boundless. Stay curious, seek out new knowledge, and remain a student of your industry and entrepreneurship at large. Your willingness to learn and evolve will keep you at the forefront of innovation and success.

Build Meaningful Connections

Entrepreneurship, though often embarked upon solo, is not a journey to be taken in isolation. The connections you build along the way, from mentors and peers to customers and collaborators, will enrich your journey immeasurably. Invest in your network, cherish your community, and remember that success is sweeter when shared.

Prioritize Your Well-being

Your business's most valuable asset is you. Prioritizing your physical, mental, and emotional well-being is not a luxury but a necessity. Balance hard work with self-care, ensuring that you are at your best. After all, a healthy entrepreneur is the cornerstone of a thriving business.

Stay True to Your Vision

In the whirlwind of entrepreneurship, it's easy to lose sight of your original vision. Regularly revisiting your 'why' can provide clarity, direction, and motivation. Stay true to the vision that sparked your entrepreneurial journey, letting it guide your decisions and inspire your actions.

Believe in Yourself

Finally, believe in yourself and your ability to make your entrepreneurial dreams a reality. Your passion, vision, and dedication have the power to transform challenges into opportunities, ideas into innovations, and dreams into tangible successes.

As you venture forward, armed with the insights and strategies outlined in this guide, remember that the world of remote work and entrepreneurship is one of limitless potential. It's a realm where creativity, perseverance, and resilience are rewarded, where challenges are the fertile ground for growth, and where every entrepreneur has the power to make a lasting impact.

Let these final words serve as a reminder of your strength, potential, and the incredible journey that lies ahead. Embrace the adventure with an open heart and an unwavering spirit, for the future is yours to shape. Here's to your continued success, growth, and the remarkable journey of entrepreneurship that awaits.

CONCLUSION

As we draw the curtains on this journey through "Home Hustle Harmony: Unlocking Your Work-From-Home Wealth," it's clear that the realm of home-based entrepreneurship is one of boundless potential and continual learning. The chapters within this book have traversed the spectrum of essential knowledge, from the foundational aspects of business setup and management to the adaptive strategies needed to thrive in an ever-evolving marketplace.

The journey of a home-based entrepreneur is both personal and professional, a delicate balance of self-discipline, innovation, and resilience. The insights and strategies outlined here are your toolkit, designed to empower you to build, grow, and sustain a successful home-based business. But the true essence of this journey lies in your hands—your actions, decisions, and unwavering commitment to your vision.

As you move forward, armed with the knowledge and insights from this guide, remember that entrepreneurship is not just about reaching a destination but about the growth, discoveries, and transformations that occur along the way. May you embrace the challenges, celebrate the victories, and continue to forge a path that is uniquely yours, filled with purpose, passion, and prosperity.